P1

Prayer

Mahatma Gandhi

₹ 100

ISBN : 978-81-7028-959-3

Edition : 2014 © Rajpal & Sons

PRAYER by Mahatma Gandhi

Printed at G.H. Prints Pvt. Ltd., Delhi

RAJPAL & SONS
1590, Madarsa Road, Kashmere Gate, Delhi-110006
Phone : 011-23869812, 23865483, Fax : 011-23867791
website : www.rajpalpublishing.com
e-mail : sales@rajpalpublishing.com

TO THE READER

I would like to say to the diligent reader of my writings and to others who are interested in them that I am not at all concerned with appearing to be consistent. In my search after Truth I have discarded many ideas and learnt many new things. Old as I am in age, I have no feeling that I have ceased to grow inwardly or that my growth will stop at the dissolution of the flesh. What I am concerned with is my readiness to obey the call of Truth, my God, from moment to moment, and, therefore, when anybody finds any inconsistency between any two writings of mine, if he has still faith in my sainty, he would do well to choose the later of the two on the same subject.

Harijan, 24-4-'33, p. 2   **M. K. Gandhi**

CONTENTS

SECTION I
Meaning of and Necessity for Prayer

What is Prayer?	13
True Prayer	14
True Worship	15
The Greatest Binding Force	15
Prayer is All Inclusive	16
Meaning of and Necessity for Prayer	16
Prayer is Necessary for All	19
Man Cannot Live Without Prayer	20
Hypocrisy of Lip-prayer	20
Why Pray?	21
The Object of Prayer	22
Spontaneous Upwelling of the Heart	23
A Man of Prayer Knows No Fear	23
Why Recite His Name?	24
Beauty of Repetition	25
No Faith in Prayer!	26
Why No Faith in Prayer?	33
Have Faith	33
God's Word	35
निबल के बल राम	35
The Only Help of the Helpless	37
God's Covenant	38
Secret of Self-control	39

A Call to Repentance	41
Visitations	42
"Inner Voice"	44

SECTION II
Forms and Methods of Prayer

Yajna	49
How I Establish Communion with God	49
The Form of My Prayer	50
Service is Prayer	51
Resign to His Will	54
How to and Whom to Pray?	56
Punctuality at Prayers	58
God's Time Never Stops	59
Never Miss Prayers	60
Attendance At Prayers	61
The Spiritual Value of Silence	63
Silent Prayers	65
Silence During Prayers	66
How I Introduced Congregational Prayer	67
Congregational Prayer	68
Co-operative Prayer	70
My Faith In Public Prayer	71
Crowds Attend My Prayers	71
Individual Prayer	71
Concentration During Prayers	73
Compulsory Prayer	74
The Malady Of Intolerance	75
Fasting and Prayer	76
The Truest Prayer	79
The Inner Meaning of the Fast	81
The Use of Images in Prayer	82
Idol-worship	83

Idolatry Vs. Idol-worship	84
Worship in Temples	85
Are Temples Necessary?	86
Are Places of Worship a Superstition?	89
Why no Temple in the Ashram?	91
A Model Temple	92
Nature's Temple of Worship	94
Tree Worship	95
Atmosphere for Prayers	97
The Place of Prayer in Ashram Life	97
The Ashram Prayer	106
About Prayer at the Ashram	109
Time Taken Up By Prayers	111
Prayers Especially for Women	112

SECTION III
Ramanama

A Good Seed Sown	121
Who is Rama?	121
Power of Ramanama	123
A Well-tried Formula	125
Ridiculing Ramanama	125
Ramanama Must Not Cease	126
Ramanama and National Service	127
Ramanama	128
References	129

SECTION I

Meaning of and Necessity for Prayer

Prayer is nothing else but an intense longing of the heart. You may express yourself through the lips; you may express yourself in the private closet or in the public; but to be genuine, the expression must come from the deepest recesses of the heart.

*

There is an eternal struggle raging in man's breast between the powers of darkness and of light, and who has not the sheet-anchor of prayer to rely upon will be a victim to the powers of darkness.

*

Begin, therefore, your day with prayer, and make it so soulful that it may remain with you until the evening. Close the day with prayer so that you may have a peaceful night free from dreams and nightmares.

SECTION 1

What is Prayer?

Prayer means asking God for something in a reverent attitude. But the word is used also to denote any devotional act. Worship is a better term to use for what the correspondent has in mind. But definition apart, what is it that millions of Hindus, Musalmans, Christians and Jews and others do every day during the time set apart for the adoration of the Maker? It seems to me that it is a yearning of the heart to be one with the Maker, an invocation for His blessing. It is in this case the attitude that matters, not words uttered or muttered.

And often the association of words that have been handed-down from ancient times has an effect which in their rendering into one's mother-tongue they will lose altogether. Thus the *Gayatri mantra* translated and recited in, say, Gujarati, will not have the same effect as the original. The utterance of the word Rama will instantaneously affect millions of Hindus, when the word God, although they may understand the meaning, will leave them untouched. Words after all acquire a power by long usage and sacredness associated with their use. There is much, therefore, to be said for the retention of old Sanskrit formulae for the most prevalent *mantras* or verses. That the meaning of them should be properly understood goes without saying.

There can be no fixed rule laid down as to the time these devotional acts should take. It depends upon individual temperament. These are precious moments in one's daily life. The exercises are intended to sober and humble us and enable us to realize that nothing happens without His will and that we are but 'clay in the hands of the Potter'. These are moments when one reviews one's immediate past, confesses one's weakness, asks for forgiveness and strength to be and do better. One minute may be enough for some, twenty-four hours may be too little for others.

For those who are filled with the presence of God in them, to labour is to pray. Their life is one continuous prayer or act of worship. For those others who act only to sin, to indulge themselves, and live for self, no time is too much. If they had patience and faith and the will to be pure, they would pray till they feel the definite purifying presence of God within them.

For us, ordinary mortals, there must be a middle path between these two extremes. We are not so exalted as to be able to say that all our acts are a dedication, nor perhaps are we so far gone as to be living purely for self. Hence have all religions set apart times for general devotion. Unfortunately these have nowadays become merely mechanical and formal, where they are not hypocritical. What is necessary, therefore, is the correct attitude to accompany these devotions.

For definite personal prayer in the sense of asking God for something, it should certainly be in one's own tongue. Nothing can be grander than to ask God to make us act justly towards everything that lives.[1]

Prayer is nothing else but an intense longing of the heart. You may express yourself through the lips; you may express yourself in the private closet or in public; but to be genuine, the expression must come from the deepest recesses of the heart.[2]

As grain is the body's food, so worship is the soul's. He who is convinced about the existence of the soul cannot live without worship. Prayer means the soul turning towards God.[3]

True Prayer

True prayer never goes unanswered. It does not mean that every little thing we ask for from God is readily given to us. It is only when we shed our selfishness with a conscious effort and approach God in true humility that our prayers find a response.

In the Ashram prayer nothing is asked. The prayer is for God to make us better men and women. If the prayer came truly from the heart, God's grace would surely descend upon us. There is not a blade of grass which moves without His will, not one single true thought which does not leave a mark on character. It is good, therefore, to develop the daily habit of prayer.⁴

True Worship

We have forgotten God and we worship Satan. A man's duty is to worship God. Telling one's beads is no symbol of that worship; neither is going to mosque or temple, nor saying the *namaz* or the *gayatri*. These things are all right as far as they go. It is necessary to do the one or the other according to one's religion. But by themselves they are no indication of one's being devoted to God in worship. He alone truly adores God who finds his happiness in the happiness of others, speaks evil of none, does not waste his time in the pursuit of riches, does nothing immoral, who acquits himself with others as with a friend, does not fear the plague or any human being.⁵

"As is the God, so is the votary", is a maxim worth considering. Its meaning has been distorted and men have gone astray...I am not likely to obtain the result flowing from the worship of God by laying myself prostrate before Satan. If, therefore, anyone were to say: "I want to worship God; it does not matter that I do so by means of Satan", it would be set down as ignorant folly. We reap exactly as we sow.⁶

We are all children of the same God. "Verily verily I say unto you, not everyone that sayeth unto me Lord, Lord, shall enter the kingdom of Heaven, but he that doeth the will of my Father which is in heaven shall enter the Kingdom", was said, though in different words, by all the great teachers of the world.⁷

The Greatest Binding Force

Prayer is the greatest binding force, making for the solidarity and oneness of the human family. If a person realizes his unity through prayer, he will look upon everybody as [t]here will be no high, no low, no narrow provincialism [r]ivalries in the matter of language between an Andhra [a Tam]ilian, a Kanarese and a Malayalee. There will be [no invidio]us distinction between a touchable and untouchable, a Hindu and a Musalman, a Parsi, a Christian or a Sikh. Similarly, there would be no scramble for personal gain or power between various groups or between different members within a group.

The outer must reflect the inner. If we are in tune with God, no matter how big a gathering, perfect quiet and order would prevail and even the weakest would enjoy perfect protection. Above all, realization must mean freedom from all earthly fear.[8]

How shall we know the (God's) will? By prayer and right living. Indeed prayer should mean right living. There is a *bhajan* we sing every day before the Ramayana commences whose refrain is "Prayer has been never known to have failed anybody. Prayer means being one with God."[9]

Prayer is All Inclusive

God does not come down in person to relieve suffering.

He works through human agency. Therefore, prayer to God, to enable one to relieve the suffering of others, must mean a longing and readiness on one's part to labour for it.

The prayer is not exclusive. It is not restricted to one's own caste or community. It is all inclusive. It comprehends the whole of humanity. Its realization would thus mean the establishment of the Kingdom of Heaven on earth.[10]

Meaning of and Necessity for Prayer

I am glad that you all want me to speak to you on the meaning of and the necessity for prayer. I believe that prayer is the very soul and essence of religion, and, therefore, prayer must be the very core of the life of man, for no man can live without religion. There are some who in the egotism of their reason declare that they have nothing to do with religion. But it is like a man saying that he breathes but that he has no nose. Whether by reason or by instinct, or by superstition, man acknowledges some sort of relationship with the divine. The rankest agnostic or atheist does acknowledge the need of a moral principle, and associates something good with its observance and something bad with its non-observance. Bradlaugh, whose atheism is well known, always insisted on proclaiming his innermost conviction. He had to suffer a lot for thus speaking the truth, but he delighted in it and said that truth is its own reward. Not that he was quite insensible to the joy resulting from the observance of truth. This joy, however, is not at all worldly, but springs out of communion with the divine. That is why I have said that even a man who disowns religion cannot and does not live without religion.

Now I come to the next thing, viz, that prayer is the very core of man's life, as it is the most vital part of religion. Prayer is either petitional or in its wider sense is inward communion. In either case the ultimate result is the same. Even when it is petitional, the petition should be for the cleansing and purification of the soul, for freeing it from the layers of ignorance and darkness that envelop it. He, therefore, who hungers for the awakening of the divine in him must fall back on prayer. But prayer is no mere exercise of words or of the ears, it is no mere repetition of empty formula. Any amount of repetition of Ramanama is futile if it fails to stir the soul. It is better in prayer to have a heart without words than words without a heart. It must be in clear response to the spirit which hungers for it. And even as a hungry man relishes a hearty meal, a hungry soul will relish a heart-felt prayer. And I am giving you a bit of my experience and that of my companions when I say that he who has experienced the magic of prayer may do without food for days together but not a single moment without prayer. For without prayer there is no inward peace.

If that is the case, some one will say, we should be offering our prayers every minute of our lives. There is no doubt about it, but we, erring mortals, who find it difficult to retire within ourselves for inward communion even for a single moment, will find it impossible to remain perpetually in communion with the divine. We, therefore, fix some hours when we make a serious effort to throw off the attachments of the world for a while, we make a serious endeavour to remain, so to say, out of the flesh. You have heard Surdas' hymn. It is the passionate cry of a soul hungering for union with the divine. According to our standards he was a saint, but according to his own he was a proclaimed sinner. Spiritually he was miles ahead of us, but he felt the separation from the divine so keenly that he has uttered that anguished cry in loathing and despair.

I have talked of the necessity for prayer, and there through I have dealt with the essence of prayer. We are born to serve our fellowmen, and we cannot properly do so unless we are wide awake. There is an eternal struggle raging in man's breast between the powers of darkness and of light, and he who has not the sheet-anchor of prayer to rely upon will be a victim to the powers of darkness. The man of prayer will be at peace with himself and with the whole world, the man who goes about the affairs of the world without a prayerful heart will be miserable and will make the world also miserable. Apart therefore from its bearing on man's condition after death, prayer has incalculable value for man in this world of the living. Prayer is the only means of bringing about orderliness and peace and repose in our daily acts. We inmates of the Ashram who came here in search of truth and for insistence on truth professed to believe in the efficacy of prayers, but had never up to now made it a matter of vital concern. We did not bestow on it the care that we did on other matters. I woke from my slumbers one day and realized that I had been woefully negligent of my duty in the matter. I have, therefore, suggested measures of stern discipline and far from being any the worse, I hope we are the better for it. For it is so obvious. Take care of the vital thing and other things will take care of themselves. Rectify one angle of a square, and the other angles will be automatically right.

Begin, therefore, your day with prayer, and make it so

soulful that it may remain with you until the evening. Close the day with prayer so that you may have a peaceful night free from dreams and nightmares. Do not worry about the form of prayer. Let it be any form, it should be such as can put us into communion with the divine. Only, whatever be the form, let not the spirit wander while the words of prayer run on out of your mouth.

If what I have said has gone home to you, you will not be at peace until you have compelled your hostel superintendents to interest themselves in your prayer and to make it obligatory. Restraint self-imposed is no compulsion. A man, who chooses the path of freedom from restraint, i.e. of self-indulgence, will be a bondslave of passions, whilst the man who binds himself to rules and restraints releases himself. All things in the universe, including the sun and the moon and the stars, obey certain laws. Without the restraining influence of these laws the world would not go on for a single moment. You, whose mission in life is service of your fellowmen, will go to pieces if you do not impose on yourselves some sort of discipline, and prayer is a necessary spiritual discipline. It is discipline and restraint that separates us from the brute. If we will be men walking with our heads erect and not walking on all fours, let us understand and put ourselves under voluntary discipline and restraint.[11]

When the mind is full of prayerful thoughts, everything in the world seems good and agreeable. Prayer is essential for progress in life.[12]

Prayer is Necessary for All

In my opinion all selfless service leads to self-purification. Economic and moral development should go hand in hand. *Atma* is that which animates the body. Realization comes through purification. Prayer is necessary for all, if food is.[13]

Man's need for prayer is as great as his need for bread. A bad man will use his ears to hear evil of others and see sinful things, but the good man says that, had he a thousand eyes and ears, he would use them to contemplate the vision of God for ever and to hear devotional songs, and employ his five thousand tongues to sing His praises. It is only after I have prayed here every day that I feel the bliss of having tasted the *amrita* of knowledge. For that man who wishes to be a real human being, *dal* and *roti* are not his food. They count little to him. His real food is prayer.[14]

There can be no manner of doubt that this universe of sentient beings is governed by a Law. If you can think of Law without its Giver, I would say that the Law is the Law-giver, that is God. When we pray to the Law we simply yearn after knowing the Law and obeying it. We become what we yearn after. Hence the necessity for prayer.[15]

The necessity of prayers is a matter of universal experience. If you have faith in them, you will feel interest in them.[16]

Man Cannot Live Without Prayer

As food is necessary for the body, prayer is necessary for the soul. A man may be able to do without food for a number of days—as Macswinney did for over 70 days—but, believing in God, man cannot, should not, live a moment without prayer. You will say that we see lots of people living without prayer. I dare say they do; but it is the existence of the brute which, for man, is worse than death. I have not the shadow of a doubt that the strife and quarrels with which our atmosphere is so full today are due to the absence of the spirit of true prayer. You will demur to the statement, I know, and contend that millions of Hindus, Musalmans and Christians do offer their prayers. It is because I had thought you would raise the objection that I used the words 'true prayer'.

Hypocrisy of Lip-prayer

The fact is, we have been offering our prayers with the lips but hardly ever with our hearts, and it is to escape, if possible, the hypocrisy of the lip-prayer, that we in the Ashram repeat every evening the last verses of the second chapter of the *Bhagavadgita*. The condition of the 'Equable in Spirit' that is described in those verses, if we contemplate, them daily, is bound slowly to turn our hearts towards God. If you would base your education on the true foundation of a pure character and pure heart, there is nothing so helpful as to offer your prayers every day, truly and religiously.[17]

Prayer is even more essential for the well-being of the soul than is food for the maintenance of the body. It becomes necessary to give up food on occasions in order to benefit the body. But prayer may never be abandoned. If we provide food for the body which is perishable, then, surely, it is our primary "duty to provide food for the soul which is imperishable, and such sustenance is found in prayer. The real meaning of prayer is devoted worship.[18]

If we believed in God,..., it followed that we must pray to Him. Though prayer, it was said, was to the soul what food was to the body, yet prayer was far more important for the soul than food was for the body, because we could at times go without food and the body would feel the better for the fast, but there was no such thing as prayer-fast. ...

We can over-indulge in food. But we can never over-indulge in prayer.[19]

Why Pray?

A friend from Baroda wrote to me :

"You ask us to pray to God to give light to the whites in South Africa and strength and courage to the Indians there to remain steadfast to the end. A prayer of this nature can only be addressed to a person. If God is an all-pervading and all-powerful force, what is the point of praying to Him? He goes on with His work whatever happens."

I have written on this topic before. But as it is a question that crops up again and again further elucidation is likely to help someone or the other. In my opinion, Rama, Rahaman, Ahurmazda, God or Krishna are all attempts on the part of

Meaning of and Necessity for Prayer

man to name that invincible force which is the greatest of all forces.

It is inherent in man, imperfect he though be, ceaselessly to strive after perfection. In the attempt he falls into reverie. And, just as a child tries to stand, falls down again and again and ultimately learns how to walk, even so man, with all his intelligence is mere infant as compared to the infinite and ageless God. This may appear to be an exaggeration but is not. Man can only describe God in his own poor language. The power we call God defies description. Nor does that power stand in need of any human effort to describe Him. It is man who requires the means whereby he can describe that Power which is vaster than the ocean.

If this premise is accepted, there is no need to ask why we pray. Mall can only conceive God within the limitations of his own mind. If God is vast and boundless as the ocean, how can a tiny drop like man imagine what He is? He can only experience what the ocean is like, if he falls into and is merged in it. This realization is beyond description. In Madame Blavatsky's language man, in praying, worships his own glorified self. He can truly pray, who has the conviction that God is within him. He who has not, need not pray. God will not be offended, but I can say from experience that he who does not pray is certainly a loser.

What matters then whether one man worships God as a Person and another as Force? Both do right according to their lights. None knows and perhaps never will know what is absolutely proper way to pray. The ideal must always remain the ideal. One need only remember that God is the Force among all the forces. All other forces are material. But God is the vital force or spirit which is all-pervading, all-embracing and therefore beyond human ken.[20]

The Object of Prayer

The object of prayer is not to please God, who does not want our prayers or praise, but to purify ourselves. The process of self-purification consists in a conscious realization of His presence within us. There is no strength greater than that which such realization gives. Presence of God has to be felt in every walk of life: If you think that as soon as you leave the prayer ground you can live and behave anyhow; your attendance of the prayer is useless.[21]

Prayer ought to result in self-purification and it ought to transmute our entire conduct. If anybody thinks that it gives him licence to do as he likes during the rest of the day, he deceives himself and others. That is a travesty of the true meaning of prayer.[22]

Prayer does for the purification of the mind what the bucket and the broom do for the cleaning up of our physical surroundings. No matter whether the prayer we recite is the Hindu prayer or the Muslim or the Parsi, its function is essentially the same, namely, purification of the heart.[23]

Spontaneous Upwelling of the Heart

Whatever measure of success I have attained in the realization of truth and non-violence is the result of prayer.

Prayer should be a spontaneous upwelling of the heart. One should not pray if one feels that the prayer is a burden. God is not hungry for man's prayer or praise. He tolerates all because He is all Love. If we feel that we owe a debt to Him, who is the giver of all things, we should remember Him and pray to Him out of sheer gratitude. The fear of incurring any body's ridicule or displeasure should never deter one from performing one's elementary duty towards the Maker.[24]

A Man of Prayer Knows No Fear

Prayer becomes a daily obligatory ritual for you. Prayer plays a large part in a self-purificatory sacrifice. The more you apply yourselves to it, the more fearlessness you will experience in daily life, for fearlessness is a sign and symbol of self-purification. I do not know a man or a woman who was on the path of self-purification and was still obsessed by fear. Generally there are two kinds of fears in men's minds-fear of death and fear or loss of material possessions. A man of prayer and self-purification will shed the fear of death and embrace death as a boon companion and will regard all earthly possessions as fleeting and of no account. He will see that he has no right to possess wealth when misery and pauperism stalk the land and when there are millions who have to go without a meal. No power on earth can subdue a man who has shed these two fears. But for that purpose the prayer should be a thing of the heart and not a thing of outward demonstration. It must take us daily nearer to God, and a prayerful man is sure to have his heart's desire fulfilled, for the simple reason that he will never have an improper desire. Continue this ritual and you will shed lustre not only on your city but on our country. I hope this brief prayer of mine will find a lodgment in your heart.[25]

Why should one fear, who knows that God is the Protector of all? By saying that God is the Protector of all I do not mean that none would be able to rob us or that no animal will attack us. It is no slur on God's protection if such things happen to us; "it is only due to out lack of faith in Him. The river is for ever ready to give water to all. But if one does not go near it with a pot to get water, or avoids it thinking its water poisonous, how can that be the fault of the river? All fear is a sign of lack of faith. But faith cannot be developed by means of reasoning. It comes gradually through quiet thinking, contemplation and practice. To develop such faith, we pray to God, read good books, seek the company of the good and take to sacrificial spinning at the wheel. He who has no faith will not even touch the spinning-wheel.[26]

Why Recite His Name?

There are many who, whether from mental laziness or from having fallen into a bad habit believe that God is and will help us unasked. Why then is it necessary to recite His name?

It is true that if God is, He is irrespective of our belief. But realization of God is infinitely more than mere belief. That can come only by constant practice. This is true of all science. How much more true of the science of all sciences?

Man often repeats the name of God parrot-wise and expects fruit from so doing. The true seeker must have that living faith which will not only dispel the untruth of parrot-wise repetition from within him but also from the hearts of others.[27]

Beauty of Repetition

"This repetition of one and the same thing over and over again jars on me. It may be the defect of my rationalist mathematical temperament. But somehow I cannot like the repetition. For instance, even Bach's wonderful music fails to appeal to me when the text 'Father, forgive them, they know not what they do,' is repeated over and over again."

"But even in mathematics, you have your recurring decimals," said Gandhiji smiling.

"But each recurs with a definite new fact," said the mathematician.

"Even so," said Gandhiji, "each repetition, or *japa* as it is called, has a new meaning, each repetition carries you nearer and nearer to God. This is a concrete fact, and I may tell you that you are here talking to no theorist, but to one who has experienced what he says every minute of his life, so much so that it is easier for the life to stop than for this incessant process to stop. It is definite need of the soul."

"I quite see it, but for the average man it becomes an empty formula."

"I agree, but the best thing is liable to be abused. There is room for any amount of hypocrisy, but even hypocrisy is an ode to virtue. And I know that for ten thousand hypocrites, you would find millions of simple souls who find their solace from it. It is like scaffolding quite essential to a building."

"But," said Pierre Ceresole, "if I may carry the simile a

Meaning of and Necessity for Prayer

little further, you agree that the scaffolding has to be removed when the building is complete?"

"Yes, it would be removed when this body is removed."

"Why?"

"Because," said Wilkinson who was closely following the discourse, "we are eternally building."

"Because," said Gandhiji, we are eternally striving after perfection. God alone is perfect, man is never perfect."[28]

This is how repetition of God's name wipes out one's sins. Anyone who sincerely follows that practice is bound to have faith. He starts with the conviction that such repetition will wipe out his sins. Wiping out of sins means self-purification. One who repeats God's name daily with faith will never grow tired of doing so, and therefore, the name which he repeats with his lip to start with sinks ultimately into his heart, and that purifies him. This is a universal experience. Psychologists also believe that man becomes what he thinks. Ramanama follows this law. I' have unshakable faith in the virtue of repeating God's name. I am convinced that the person who discovered it had first-hand experience [of spiritual life] and that his discovery is of the utmost value. The door of purification should open even 'for the illiterate. Repetition of God's name opens it for them. (See Gita IX, 22, X. 10). Telling beads and similar practices help one to concentrate and to count the number of times the name has been repeated.[29]

No Faith in Prayer!

I

Here is a letter written by a student to the Principal of a national institution, asking to be excused from attending its prayer meetings:

"I beg to state that I have no belief in prayer, as I do not believe in anything known as God to which I should pray. I never feel any necessity of supposing a God for myself. What do I lose if I do not care for Him, and calmly and sincerely work my own schemes?

"So far as congregational prayer is concerned, it is of no use. Can such a huge mass of men enter into any mental concentration upon a thing, however trifling it may be? Are the little and ignorant children expected to fix their fickle attention on the subtlest ideas of our great scriptures, God and soul and equality of all men and many other high-sounding phrases? This great performance is required to be done at a particular time at the command of a particular man, Can love for the so-called Lord take its root in the hearts of boys by any such mechanical function? Nothing can be more repugnant to reason than to expect the same behaviour from men of every temperament. Therefore, prayer should not be a compulsion. Let those pray who have a taste forit, and those avoid who dislike it. Anything done without conviction is an immoral and degrading action."

Let us first examine the worth of the last idea. Is it an immoral and degrading act to submit to discipline before one begins to have conviction about its necessity? Is it immoral and degrading to study subjects according to the school syllabus, if one has no conviction about its utility? May a boy be excused from studying his vernacular, if he has persuaded himself that it is useless? Is it not truer to say that a school boy has no conviction about the things he has to learn, or the discipline he has to go through? His choice is exhausted, if he had it, when he elected to belong to an institution. His joining one means that he will willingly submit to its rules and regulations. It is open to him to leave it, but he may not choose what or how he will learn.

It is for teachers to make attractive and intelligible, what to the pupils may, at first, appear repulsive or uninteresting.

It is easy enough to say : "I do not believe in God."

For, God permits all things to be said of Him with impunity. He looks at our acts. And any breach of His Law carries with it, not its vindictive, but its purifying, compelling, punishment. God's existence cannot be, does not need to be proved. God is. If He is not felt, so much the worse for us. The absence of feeling is a disease which we shall some day throw off *nolens volens*.

But a boy may not argue. He must, out of sense of

discipline, attend prayer meetings, if the institution to which he belongs requires such attendance. He may respectfully put his doubts before his teachers. He need not believe what does not appeal to him. But if he has respect for his teachers, he will do without believing what he is asked to do, not out of fear, nor out of churlishness, but with the knowledge that it is right for him so to do, and with the hope that what is dark to him today will some day be made clear to him.

Prayer is not an asking. It is a longing of the soul. It is a daily admission of one's weakness. The tallest among us has a perpetual reminder of his nothingness before death, disease, old age, accidents etc. We are living in the midst of death. What is the value of 'working for our own schemes' when they might be reduced to naught in the twinkling of an eye, or when we may, equally swiftly and unawares, be taken away from them? But we may feel strong as a rock, if we could truthfully say: 'We work for God and His schemes.' Then, all is as clear as day-light. Then, nothing perishes. All perishing is, then, only what seems. Death and destruction have then, *but only then,* no reality about them. For, death and destruction is then but a change. An artist destroys his picture for creating a better one. A watchmaker throws away a bad spring to put in a new and a useful one.

A congregational prayer is a mighty thing. What we do not often do alone, we do together. Boys do not need conviction. If they merely attend in obedience to the call to prayer, without inward resistance, they feel the exaltation. But many do not. They are even mischievous. All the same the unconscious effect cannot be resisted. Are there not boys who at the commencement of their career were scoffers, but who subsequently became mighty believers in the efficacy of congregational prayer? It is a common experience for men, who have no robust faith, to seek the comfort of congregational prayer. All who flock to churches, temples, or mosques are not scoffers or humbugs. They are honest men and women. For them congregational prayer is like a daily bath, a necessity of their existence. These places of worship are not a mere idle superstition to be swept away at the first opportunity. They have survived all attacks up to now, and are likely to persist to the end of time.[30]

II

A correspondent thus writes on my article "No Faith in Prayer!"

"In your article bearing the above caption, you hardly do justice to the 'boy' or to your own position as a great thinker. It is true that the expressions used by the writer in his letter are not all happy, but of his clarity of thought there is no doubt. It is also very evident that he is not a boy as the word is understood. I should be much surprised to find him under twenty. Even if he is young, he seems to show sufficient intellectual development, not to be treated in the manner of 'a boy may not argue'. The writer of the letter is a rationalist while you are a believer, two age-old types with age-old conflict. The attitude of the one is, 'Let me be convinced and I shall believe', that of the other is, 'Believe and conviction shall come'. The first appeals to reason, the second appeals to authority. You seem to think that agnosticism is but a passing phase among all young people, and that faith comes to them sooner or later. There is the well-known case of Swami Vivekananda to support your view. You, therefore, proceed to prescribe a compulsory dose of prayer to the 'boy' for his own good. Your reasons are twofold. Firstly, prayer for its own sake, as a recognition of one's own littleness, and mightiness and goodness of the supposed higher being. Secondly, for its utility, for the solace it brings to those who want to be solaced. I shall dispose of the second argument first. Here, it is recommended as a sort of staff to the weak. Such are the trials of life, and such is their power to shatter reason of men that great many people may need prayer and faith some time. They have a right to it and they are welcome to it. But there have been, and there are always, some true rationalists—few, no doubt—who have never felt the necessity of either. There is also the class of people who, while they are not aggressive doubters, are indifferent to religion.

"As all people do not ultimately require the help of prayer, and as those who feel its necessity are *free* to take to it, and do take to it when required, compulsion in prayer, from the point of utility cannot be upheld. Compulsory physical exercise and education may be necessary for physical and mental development of a person, not so the belief in God and prayer for the moral side. Some of the world's greatest agnostics have been the most moral men. To these, I suppose, you would recommend prayer for its own sake, as an expression of humility, in fact, your first argument. Too much has been made of this humility. So vast is knowledge that even the greatest scientists have felt humble sometimes, but their general trait has been that of *masterful* enquiry, their faith in their own powers has been as great as their conquest of nature. Had it not been so, we shall still be scratching earth with bare fingers for roots, nay, we should have been wiped out of the surface of the earth.

"During the Ice Age, when human beings were dying of cold and fire was first discovered, your prototype in that age must have taunted the discoverer with: "What is the use of your schemes, of what avail are they against the power and wrath of God?' The humble have been promised the Kingdom of God hereafter. We do not know whether they will get it, but here on this earth their portion is serfdom. To revert to the main point, your assertion about 'accept the belief and the faith shall come' is too true, terribly true. Much of religious fanaticism of this world can be traced directly to this' kind of teaching. Provided you catch them young enough, you can make a good majority of human beings believe *in anything*. That is how your orthodox Hindu, or fanatical Mahomedan, is manufactured. There are, of course, always a small few in either community who will outgrow these beliefs that have been forced upon them. Do you know that if the Hindus and the Mahomedans stopped studying their scriptures, until they reached maturity, they would not be such fanatical believers in their dogmas, and would cease to quarrel for their sake? Secular education is the remedy for Hindu-Muslim riots, but you are not made that way.

"Great as our debt is to you for setting an unprecedented example in courage, action and sacrifice in this country where people have been always much afraid, when the final judgment is passed on your work, it will be said that your influence gave a great setback to intellectual progress in this country."

I do not know the meaning of boy 'as the word is ordinarily

understood', if a 20 year old lad is not a boy. Indeed, I would call all school-going persons boys and girls, irrespective of their ages. But whether the doubting student may be called a boy or a man, my arguments. must stand. A student is like a soldier (and a soldier may be 40 years old) who may not argue about matters of discipline, when he has put himself and chooses to remain under it. A soldier may not remain a unit in his regiment and have the option of doing or not doing things he is a asked to do. Similarly, a student, no matter how wise or old he is, surrenders when he joins a school or a college the right of rejecting its discipline. Here, there is no underrating or despising the intelligence of the student. It is an aid to his intelligence for him to come voluntarily under discipline. But my correspondent willingly bears the heavy yoke of the tyranny of words. He scents 'compulsion' in every act that displeases the doer. But there is compulsion and compulsion. We call self-imposed compulsion self-restraint. We hug it and grow under it. But compulsion to be shunned even at the cost of life, is restraint, superimposed upon us against our wills, and often with the object of humiliating us and robbing us of our dignity as men and boys, if you will. Social restraints generally are healthy, and we reject them to our own undoing. Submission to crawling orders is unmanly and cowardly. Worse still is the submission to the multitude of passions that crowd round us every moment of our lives, ready to hold us their slaves.

But the correspondent has yet another word that holds him in its chains. It is the mighty word 'rationalism'. Well, I had a full dose of it. Experience has humbled me enough to let me realize the specific limitations of reason. Just as matter misplaced becomes dirt, reason misused becomes lunacy. If we would but render unto Caesar that which is Caesar's, all would be well.

Rationalists are admirable beings. Rationalism is a hideous monster when it claims for itself omnipotence. Attribution of omnipotence to reason is as bad a piece of idolatry as is worship of stock and stone, believing it to be God.

Who has reasoned out the use of prayer? Its use is felt after practice. Such is the world's testimony. Cardinal Newman never surrendered his reason, but he yielded a better place to prayer when he humbly sang: 'One step enough for me'. Shankara was a prince among reasoners. There is hardly anything in the world's literature to surpass Shankara's rationalism. But he yielded the first place to prayer and faith.

The correspondent has made a hasty generalization from the fleeting and disturbing events that are happening before us. But everything on this earth lends itself to abuse. It seems to be a law governing everything pertaining to man. No doubt, religion has to answer for some of the most terrible crimes in history. But that is the fault not of religion, but of the ungovernable brute in man. He has not yet shed the effects of his brute ancestry.

I do not know a single rationalist who has never done anything in simple faith, and has based every one of his acts on reason. But we all know millions of human beings, living their more or less orderly lives because of their childlike faith in the Maker of us all. That very faith is a prayer. The 'boy', on whose letter I based my article, belongs to that vast mass of humanity, and the article was written to steady him and his fellow-searchers, not to disturb the happiness of rationalists like the correspondent.

But he quarrels even with the bent that is given to the youth of the world by their elders and teachers. But that, it seems, is an inseparable handicap (if it be one) of impressionable age. Purely secular education is also an attempt to mould the young mind after a fashion. The correspondent is good enough to grant that the body and the mind may be trained and directed. Of the soul, which makes the body and the mind possible, he has no care or perhaps he is in doubt as to its existence. But this belief cannot avail him. He cannot escape the consequence of his reasoning. For, why may not a believer argue, on the correspondent's own ground, and say he must influence the soul of boys and girls, even as the others influence the body and the intelligence? The evils of religious' instructions will vanish with the evolution of the true religious spirit. To give up religious instruction is like letting a field lie fallow, and grow weeds for want of the' tiller's knowledge of the proper use of the field.

The correspondent's excursion into the great discoveries of the ancients is really irrelevant to the subject under discussion. No one questions, I do not, the utility or the brilliance of those discoveries. They were generally a proper field for the use and exercise of reason. But they, the ancients, did not delete from their lives the predominant function of faith and prayer. Works without faith and prayer, are like an artificial flower that has no fragrance. I plead, not for the suppression of reason, but for a due recognition of that in us which sanctifies reason itself.[31]

Why No Faith in Prayer?

And why no faith in prayer? Faith is either derived or revealed from within. You should derive it from the testimony without exception of all the teachers and the seers of all climes, countries and times. A true prayer is not a mere lip expression. It need never lie. Selfless service is prayer. You must not say, 'I have no faith in prayer.'[32]

Have Faith

Visitor: "If you pray to God, can He intervene and set aside the law for your sake?"

Gandhiji: "God's law remains unaltered but since that very law says that every action has a result, if a person prays, his prayer is bound to produce an unforeseeable result in terms of His law..."

"But do you know the God to whom you pray?"

"No, I don't."

"To whom shall we pray then?"

"To the God whom we do not know—we do not always know the person to whom we pray."

"May be, but the person to whom we pray is knowable."

"So is God; and since He is knowable, we search. It may

Meaning of and Necessity for Prayer

take a billion years before we find Him. What does it matter? So, I say, even if you do not believe, you must continue to pray, i.e., search. 'Help thou my unbelief' is a verse from the Bible to be remembered. But it is not right to ask such questions. You must have infinite patience, and inward longing. Inward longing obviates all such questions. 'Have faith and you will be whole' is another tip from the Bible."

"When I look at nature around me," the venerable visitor finally said, "I say to myself, there must be one Creator, one God and to Him I should pray."

"That again is reasoning," Gandhiji replied. "God is beyond reason. But I have nothing to say if your reason is enough to sustain you."[33]

To quote from scriptures will not help you. Draupadi's prayer is a celebrated instance. If one has faith in one's prayer, I have not a shadow of a doubt in my mind that it can move mountain. Faith and proof are contradictory acts. Hence illustrations are of little avail. The only thing is to pray whether one gets an answer to one's prayer or not. Prayer should never be directed to a selfish object.[34]

I can give you no help if you have no faith in God, and if you have faith in God you need no help from me. Therefore I would advise you to have faith in God and therefore also in prayer. You will then find that all the evil thoughts will leave you and that you will find peace of mind gradually growing on you, and you will become a fit instrument for service.[35]

I understand your view about the ceremonial recitation of the Gita. On this issue you may quarrel with Kakasaheb to your heart's content. Personally, I think that at the back of your opposition to the proposal is your aversion to or lack of faith in the prayers themselves. If you had your way, I think you would have nothing besides the *dhun*. I would advise you to have faith in all the items of the prayers. If possible, concentrate your attention on the meaning of each item. If you cannot do that, have faith that the words you hear are noble and that even the fact of listening to them will do you good, and attend to them respectfully. Please do not understand from this that I wish to convert you to the proposal for completing the recitation in seven days. I have written this to convince you that there is some meaning in the prayers behind which lies fifteen years' *tapascharya*, with unswerving faith, on the part of some of us.[36]

God's Word

My success lies in my continuous, humble, truthful striving. I *know* the path. It is straight and narrow. It is like the edge of a sword. I rejoice to walk on it. I weep when I slip. God's word is: "He who strives never perishes". I have implicit faith in that promise. Though therefore from my weakness I fail a thousand times, I will not lose faith but hope that I shall see the Light when the flesh has been brought under perfect subjection as some day it must.[37]

निर्बल के बल राम

Though I had acquired a nodding acquaintance with Hinduism and other religions of the world, I should have known that it would not be enough to save me in my trials. Of the thing that sustains him through trials man has no inkling, much less knowledge, at the time. If an unbeliever, he will attribute his safety to chance. If a believer, he will say God saved him. He will conclude, as well he may, that his religious study or spiritual discipline was at the back of the state of grace within him. But in the hour of his deliverance he does not know whether his spiritual discipline or something else saves him. Who that has prided himself on his spiritual strength has not seen it humbled to the dust? A knowledge of religion, as distinguished from experience, seems but chaff in such moments of trial.

It was in England that I first discovered the futility of mere religious knowledge. How I was saved on previous occasions is more than I can say, for I was very young then;

but now I was twenty and had gained some experience as husband and father.

During the last year, as far as I can remember, of my stay in England, that is in 1890, there was a Vegetarian Conference at Portsmouth to which an Indian friend and I were invited. Portsmouth is a sea-port with a large naval population. It has many houses with women of ill fame, women not actually prostitute, but at the same time, not very scrupulous about their morals. We were put up in one of these houses. Needless to say, the Reception Committee did not know anything about it. It would have been difficult in a town like Portsmouth to find out which were good lodgings and which were bad for occasional travellers like us.

We returned from the Conference in the evening. After dinner we sat down to play a rubber of bridge, in which our landlady joined, as is customary in England even in respectable households. Every player indulges in innocent jokes as a matter of course, but here my companion and our hostess began to make indecent ones as well. I did not know that my friend was an adept in the art. It captured me and I also joined in. Just when I was about to go beyond the limit, leaving the cards and the game to themselves, "God through the good companion uttered the blessed warning: 'Whence this devil in you, my boy? Be off, quick!'

I was ashamed. I took the warning and expressed within myself gratefulness to my friend. Remembering the vow I had taken before my mother, I fled from the scene. To my room I went quaking, trembling, and with beating heart, like a quarry escaped from its pursuer.

I recall this as the first occasion on which a woman, other than my wife, moved me to lust. I passed that night sleeplessly, all kinds of thoughts assailing me. Should I leave this house? Should I run away from the place? Where was I? What would happen to me if I had not my wits about me? I decided to act thenceforth with great caution; not to leave the house, but somehow leave Portsmouth. The Conference was not to go on for more than two days, and I remember I left Portsmouth the next evening, my companion staying there some time longer.

I did not then know the essence of religion or of God, and how He works in us. Only vaguely I understood that God had saved me on that occasion. On all occasions of trial He has saved me. I know that the phrase 'God saved me' has a deeper meaning for me today, and still I feel that I have not yet grasped its entire meaning. Only richer experience can help me to a fuller understanding. But in all my trials-of a spiritual nature, as a lawyer, in conducting institutions, and in politics-I can say that God saved me. 'When every hope is gone, 'when helpers fail and comforts flee,' I find that help arrives somehow, from I know not where. Supplication, worship, prayer tire no superstition; they are acts more real than the acts of eating, drinking, sitting or walking. It is no exaggeration to say that they alone are real, all else is unreal.

Such worship or prayer is no flight of eloquency; it is no lip-homage. It springs from the heart. If, therefore, we achieve that purity of the heart when it is 'emptied of all but love', if we keep all the chords in proper tune, they 'trembling pass in music out of sight'. Prayer needs no speech. It is in itself independent of any sensuous effort. I have not the slightest doubt that prayer is an unfailing means of cleansing the heart of passions. But it must be combined with the utmost humility.[38]

The Only Help of the Helpless

I know from correspondence with the students all over India what wrecks they have become by having stuffed their brains with information derived from a cartload of books. Some have become unhinged, others have become lunatics, some have been leading a life of helpless immaturity. My heart goes out to them when they say that try as much as they might, they are what they are, because they cannot overpower the devil. "Tell us," they plaintively ask, "how to get rid of the devil, how to get rid of the impurity that has seized us." When I ask them to take Ramanama and kneel before God and seek His help, they come to me and say, "We do not know where God is. We do not know what it is to pray." That is the state to which they have been reduced. I have, therefore, been asking the students to be on their guard.... Never own a defeat in a sacred cause and make up your minds henceforth that you *will* be pure and that you *will* find a response from God. But God never answers the prayers of the arrogant, nor the prayers of those who bargain with Him. Have you heard the story of *Gajendra Moksha*? I ask the Burmese students here who do not know one of the greatest of all poems, one of the divinest things of the world, to learn it from their Indian friends. A Tamil saying has always remained in my memory and it means, God is the help of the helpless. If you would ask Him to help you, you would go to Him in all your nakedness, approach Him without reservations, also without fear or doubts as to how He can help a fallen being like you. He who has helped millions, who have approached Him, is He going to desert you? He makes no exceptions whatsoever and you will find that everyone of your prayers will be answered. The prayer of even the most impure will be answered. I am telling this out of my personal experience, I have gone through the purgatory. Seek first the Kingdom of Heaven and everything will be added unto you.[39]

God's Covenant

You will wonder why I consented to have a prayer meeting in Bombay, when even the existence of God is with many a matter of doubt. There are others who say: 'If God is seated in the heart of everyone, who shall pray to whom, who shall invoke whom?' I am not here to solve these intellectual puzzles. I can only say that ever since my childhood prayer has been my solace and my strength.

...There are those who are struck with doubt and despair. For them there is the name of God. It is God's covenant that whoever goes to Him in weakness and helplessness, him He will make strong. 'When I am weak, then I am strong.' As the poet Surdas has sung, Rama is the strength of the weak. This strength is not to be obtained by taking up arms or by similar means. It is to be had by throwing oneself on His name. Rama is but a synonym of God. You may say God or Allah or whatever other name you like, but the moment you trust naught but Him, you are strong, all disappointment disappears.

The hymn alludes to the story of the Lord of elephants who was in the jaws of a crocodile and who had been all but drowned in water. There was only the tip of his trunk left above water when he invoked God's name and he was saved. No doubt it is an allegory. But it conceals a truth: Over and over again in my life have I found it. Even in darkest despair, when there seems no helper and no comfort in the 'wide wide world His name inspires us with strength and puts all doubts and despair to flight. The sky may be overcast today with clouds, but a fervent prayer to Him is enough to dispel them. It is because of prayer that I have known no disappointment. ... Let us pray that He may cleans our hearts of pettinesses, meannesses and deceit, and He will surely answer our prayers.[40]

Secret of Self-control

I am inundated with letters from young men who write frankly about their evil habits and about the void that their unbelief has made in their lives. No mere medical advice can bring them relief. I can only tell them that there is no way but that of surrender to and trust in God and His grace. Let us all utilize this occasion by giving the living religion in our lives the place it deserves. Has not Akhobhagat said,

> Live as you will, but so
> As to realize God.[41]

Moksha is liberation from impure thought. Complete extinction of impure thought is impossible without ceaseless penance. There is only one way to achieve this. The moment an impure thought arises, confront it with a pure one. This is possible only with God's grace, and God's grace comes through ceaseless communion with Him and complete self-surrender. This communion may in the beginning be just a lip repetition of His name even disturbed by impure thoughts.

But ultimately what is on the lips will possess the heart. And there is another thing to bear in mind. The mind may wander, but let not the senses wander with it. If the senses wander where the mind takes them, one is done for. But he who keeps control of the physical senses will some day be able to bring impure thoughts under control. . . . Impure thoughts need not dismay you. We are monarchs of the domain of Effort. God is sole Monarch of the domain of Result .... You know what to do to create a pure atmosphere about you. Spare diet, sight fixed on the earth below, and impatience with oneself to the extent of plucking the eye out if 'it offends thee'.[42]

For me the observance of even bodily *brahmacharya* has been full of difficulties. Today I may say that I feel myself fairly safe, but I have yet to achieve complete mastery over thought, which is so essential. Not that the will or effort is lacking, but it is yet a problem to me wherefrom undesirable thoughts spring their insidious invasions. I have no doubt that there is a key to lock out undesirable thoughts, but everyone has to find it out for himself. Saints and seers have left their experiences for us, but they have given us no infallible and universal prescription. For perfection or freedom from error comes only from grace, and so seekers after God have left us mantras, such as Ramanama, hallowed by their own austerities and charged with their purity. Without an unreserved surrender to His grace, complete mastery over thought is impossible. This is the teaching of every great book of religion, and I am realizing the truth of it every moment of my striving after that perfect *brahmacharya*.[43]

* * *

Prayer and *brahmacharya* are not things of the same kind. *Brahmacharya* is one of the five cardinal vows, and prayer is a means of being able to observe them. I have said a great deal to explain the necessity of *brahmacharya*. But when I tried to think, how one can observe it, I discovered a powerful means in prayer. For him who has realized the value of prayer and is able to pray with concentration, *brahmacharya* becomes quite easy to observe.[44]

There is however a golden rule for gaining control of the carnal desire. It is the repetition of the divine word 'Rama' or such other mantra. The Dwadash Mantra (ॐ नमो भगवते वासुदेवाय। A sacred incantation of these 12 letters) also serves the same purpose. Everyone must select the mantra after his heart. I have suggested the word 'Rama' because I was brought up to repeat it in my childhood and I have ever got strength and sustenance out of it. Whichever mantra is selected, one should be identified with it whilst repeating it. I have not the least doubt of ultimate success as a result of repetition of some such mantra in complete faith, even though other thoughts distract the mind. The mantra will be the light of one's life and will keep one from all distress. Such holy mantras should obviously never be used for material ends. If their use is strictly restricted to the preservation of morals, the results attained will be startling. Of course a mere repetition of such a mantra parrotwise would be of no avail. One should throw his whole soul into it. The parrot rsepeats it like a machine. We should repeat it with a view to preventing the approach 'Of unwelcome thoughts and with full faith in the efficacy 'Of the mantra to that end.[45]

It (real self-control) does not come by reading. It comes only by definite realization that God is with us and looks after us as if He had no other care besides. How this happens I do not know. That it does happen I do know. Those who have faith have all their cares lifted off their shoulders. You cannot have faith and tension at the same time.[46]

This control is unattainable save the grace of God. There is a verse in the second chapter of the Gita which freely rendered means: "sense-objects remain in abeyance whilst one is fasting or whilst the particular sense is starved, but the hankering does not cease except when one sees God face to face.[47]

A Call to Repentance

To err is human. By confessing, 'we convert our mistakes into stepping stones for advance. On the contrary, a person who tries to hide his mistakes becomes a living fraud and sinks down. Man is neither brute nor God, but a creature of God

Meaning of and Necessity for Prayer

striving to realize his divinity. Repentance and self-purification are the means. The moment we repent and ask God for forgiveness for our lapse, we are purged of our sin and new life begins for us. True repentance is an essential pre-requisite of prayer.

Prayer is not mere lip service. It must express itself through action.[48]

God does not fail to forgive even those who atone for their sins during the last moments of their life. We must have at heart the welfare of all living beings that exist on the earth, however small or large. To foster this spirit we must daily offer our prayers to the Almighty both in the morning and in the evening. The wishes for the well-being of all also embrace our own welfare.[49]

Visitations

When a man is down, he prays to God to lift him up. He is the Help of the helpless, says a Tamil proverb. The appalling disaster in Quetta paralyses one. It baffles all attempt at reconstruction. The whole truth about the disaster will perhaps never be known. The dead cannot be recalled to life.

Human effort must be there always. Those who are left behind must have help. Such reconstruction as is possible will no doubt be undertaken. All this and much more along the same line can never be a substitute for prayer.

But why pray at all? Does not God, if there be One, know what has happened? Does He stand in need of prayer to enable Him to do His duty?

No, God needs no reminder. He is within everyone. Nothing happens without His permission. Our prayer is a heart search. It is a reminder to ourselves that we are helpless without His support. No effort is complete without prayer—without a definite recognition that the best human endeavour is of no effect if it has not God's blessing behind it. Prayer is a call to humility. It is a call to self-purification, to inward search.

I must repeat what I said at the time of the Bihar disaster. There is a divine purpose behind every physical calamity. That perfected science will one day be able to tell us beforehand when earthquakes will occur, as it tells us today of eclipses, is quite possible. It will be another triumph of the human mind. But such triumphs even indefinitely multiplied can bring about no purification of self without which nothing is of any value.

Of course we will forget this latest calamity as we have forgotten the Bihar one. I ask those who appreciate the necessity of inward purification to join in the prayer that we may read the purpose of God behind such visitations, that they may humble us and prepare us to face our Maker whenever the call comes, and that we may be ever ready to share the sufferings of our fellows whoever they may be.[50]

The few lines that I wrote inviting the people to prayer and repentance on the Quetta disaster have given rise to some private correspondence. One of the correspondents asks: "At the time of the Bihar quake you had no hesitation in saying that it was to be taken by Savarna Hindus as a fit punishment for the sin of untouchability. For what sin must the more terrible '"quake of Quetta be?" The writer had the right to put the question. What I said about Bihar was deliberately said even as the lines on Quetta were deliberately written.

This call to prayer is a definite yearning of the soul. Prayer is a sign of repentance, a desire to become better, purer. A man of prayer regards what are known as physical calamities as divine chastisement. It is a chastisement alike for individuals and for nations. All chastisements do not equally startle people. Some affect only individuals, some others affect groups or nations only mildly. Disasters like Quetta stun us. Familiarity with ordinary everyday calamities breeds contempt for them. If earthquakes were a daily occurrence, we would take no notice of them. Even this Quetta one has not caused in us the same disturbance that the Bihar one did.

But it is the universal experience that every calamity brings a sensible man down on his knees. He 'thinks that it is God's answer to his sins and that he must henceforth behave better. His sins have left him hopelessly weak, and in his

Meaning of and Necessity for Prayer

weakness he cries out to God for help. Thus have millions of human beings used their personal calamities for self-improvement. Nations have been known to invoke the assistance of God when calamities have overtaken them. They have abased themselves before God and appointed days of humiliation, prayer and purification.

I have suggested nothing new or original. In these days of fashionable disbelief, it does need some courage to call men and women to repentance. But I can claim no credit for courage. For my weaknesses or idiosyncrasies are well known. If I had known Quetta, as I know Bihar and Biharis, I would certainly have mentioned the sins of Quetta, though they might be no more its specialities than untouchability was Bihar's. But we all—the rulers and the ruled—know that we have many sins personal and national to answer for. The call is to all these to repentance, prayer and humiliation. True prayer is not a prelude to inaction. It is a spur to ceaseless, selfless action. Purification is never for the selfishly idle, it accrues only to the selflessly industrious.[51]

Our forefathers and our mothers have taught us to think that, when a calamity descends upon us, it comes because of our personal sin. You know that when rain does not come in time, we perform sacrifices and ask God to forgive us our sins. It is not only here, but I have seen it in England and South Africa that, when locusts descend upon fields or any such thing happens, they appoint days of humiliation, prayer and fasting and pray for the passing of the visitation.[52]

"Inner Voice"

The "inner voice" is something which cannot be described in words. But sometimes we have a positive feeling that something in us prompts us to do a certain thing. The time when I learnt to recognise this voice was, I may say, the time when I started praying regularly. That is, it was about 1906. I searched my memory and tell you this because you asked the question. In fact, however, there was no moment when I suddenly felt that I had some new experience. I think my spiritual life has grown without my being conscious of the fact in the same way as hair grows on our body.[53]

There is something within me impelling me to cry out my agony. I have known exactly what to do. That something which never deceives me tells me now: "You have to stand against the whole world although you may have to stand alone. You have to stare the world in the face although the world may look at you with bloodshot eyes. Do not fear. Trust that little thing in you which resides in the heart and says: 'Forsake friends, wife, all; but testify to that for which you have lived and for which you have to die.'[54]

SECTION II

Forms and Methods of Prayer

Prayer brings a peace, a strength and a consolation that nothing else can give. But it must be offered from the heart. When it is not offered from the heart, it is like the beating of a drum, or Just the vocal effect of the throat sounds. When it is offered from the heart, it has the power to melt" mountains of misery. Those who want are welcome to try its" power.

I would urge the modem generation not to regard" fasting and prayer with scepticism or distrust. The greatest teachers of the world have derived extraordinary powers for the good of humanity and attained clarity of vision through fasting and prayer. Much of this discipline runs to waste because instead of being matter of the heart, it is often resorted to for stage effect.

Yajna

Now to offer prayers is easy enough. But they are not heard unless they are offered from a pure and contrite heart. Let me tell you that yajna has a deeper meaning than the offering of ghee and other things in the sacrificial fire. Yajna is sacrifice of one's all for the good of humanity, and to me these offerings of *ahutis* have a symbolic meaning. We have to offer up our weaknesses, our passions, our narrowness into the purifying fire, so that we may be cleansed. Then and then only our prayers would be heard.

Let me also place before you another aspect of prayer. You have assembled here for the fulfilment of your desires, and the *yajna* is performed to that purpose. Now desires may be good and bad, and not everyone of us knows which of his desires is good and pure and which not. It is He who presides over our thoughts and acts who knows this, and so I always pray that God may grant only such of my desires as may be good and pure, and reject all my prayers if they partake of impurity or grossness. I invite you to join me in that kind of prayer today.

One last thing. The prayer for peace is accepted on all hands as a pure prayer; and in these times of severe strife and cruel bloodshed it is well that we offer prayers for peace. There is a great Vedic prayer which I should like to recite in this connection, and I am sure you will all join me when I do so:

यदिह घोरं यदिह क्रूरं यदिह पापं।
तच्छान्तं तच्छिवं सर्वमेव शमस्तु नः॥

(Whatever there is heinous, and cruel and sinful, may all that be stilled; may everything be good and peaceful for us.)[1]

How I Establish Communion with God

I do not know whether I am a Karmayogi or any other Yogi.

Forms and Methods of Prayer **49**

I know that I cannot live without work. I crave to die with my hand at the spinning wheel. If one has to establish communion with God through some means, why not through the spinning wheel? "Him who worships Me;" says the Lord in the Gita, "I guide along the right path and see to his needs." My God is myriad-formed, and while sometimes I see Him in the spinning wheel, at other times I see Him in communal unity, then again in removal of untouchability; and that is how 1 establish communion with Him according as the Spirit moves me.²

The Form of My Prayer

A missionary who called on Gandhiji at his retreat in Segaon asked him, "What is your method of worship?"

In reply, Gandhiji said: "We have joint worship morning and evening at 4-20 a.m. and 7 p.m. This has gone on for years. We have a recitation of verses from the Gita and other accepted religious books, also hymns of saints with or without music. Individual worship cannot be described in words. It goes on continuously and even unconsciously. There is not a moment when I do not feel the presence of a witness whose eye misses nothing and with whom I strive to keep in tune. I do not pray as Christian friends do. Not because I think there is any thing wrong in it, but because words won't come to me. I suppose it is a matter of habit."

Missionary: Is there any place for supplication in your prayer?

Gandhiji: There is and there is not. God knows and anticipates our wants. The Deity does not need my supplication, but I, a very imperfect human being, do need His protection as a child that of its father. And yet I know that nothing I do is going to change His plans. You may call me a fatalist, if you like.

Missionary: Do you find any response to your prayer?

Gandhiji: I consider myself a happy man in that respect. I have never found Him lacking in response. I have found

Him nearest at hand when the horizon seemed darkest—in my ordeals in jails when it was not all smooth sailing for me. I cannot recall a moment in my life when I had a sense of desertion by God.³

1. When I pray, 1 do not ask for anything: but I simply think of some of the verses or hymns which I fancy for the moment.

2. The relation between God and myself is not only at prayer but, at all times, that of master and slave in perpetual bondage.

3. Prayer is to me the intense longing of the heart to merge myself in the Master. If a man does not pray, evidently he has no longing; there is no feeling of helplessness and when there is no helplessness, there is no need for help.⁴

Service is Prayer

If I found myself entirely absorbed in the service of the community, the reason behind it was my desire for self-realization. I had made the religion of service my own, as I felt that God could be realized only through service. And service for me was the service of India, because it came to me without my seeking, because I had an aptitude for it. I had gone to South Africa for travel, for finding an escape from Kathiawad intrigues and for gaining my own livelihood. But as I have said, I found myself in search of God and striving for self-realization.⁵

What I want to achieve—what I have been striving and pining to achieve these thirty years—is self-realization, to see God face to face, to attain *moksha*. I live and move and have my being in pursuit of this goal. All that I do by way of speaking and writing, and all my ventures in the political field, are directed to this same end.⁶

I never asked my audience to substitute the spinning wheel for the rosary. I only suggested that they could go on spinning taking the name of Narayana simultaneously. And whilst today the whole country is on fire, I think it behoves

Forms and Methods of Prayer 51

us all to fill the buckets of the spinning wheel with the water of yarn and extinguish the fire with the name of Narayana on our lips.

* * *

Narasimha Mehta does indeed sing the praise of the rosary, and the praise is well merited where it is given. But the same Narasimha has sung:

> "Of what avail is the tilak and the tulsi, of what avail is the rosary and the muttering of the Name, what avail is the grammatical interpretation of the Veda, what avail is the mastery of the letters? All these are devices to fill the belly and nothing worth without their helping to a realization of the *Para-Brahma*."

The Musalman does count the beads of his *tasbih*, and the Christian of the rosary. But both would think themselves fallen from religion if their *tasbih* and rosary prevented them from running to the succour of one who, for instance, was lying stricken with a snake-bite. Mere knowledge of the Vedas cannot make our Brahmanas spiritual preceptors. If it did, Max Muller would have become one. The Brahmana who has understood the religion of today will certainly give Vedic learning a secondary place and propagate the religion of the spinning wheel, relieve the hunger of the millions of his starving countrymen and only then, and not until then, lose himself in Vedic studies.

I have certainly regarded spinning superior to the practice of denominational religions. But that does not mean that the latter should be given up. I only mean that a Dharma which has to be observed by the followers of all religions transcends them, and hence I say that a Brahmana is a better Brahmana, a Musalman a better Musalman, a Vaishnava a better Vaishnava, if he turns the wheel in the spirit of service.

I certainly did not repeat the divine word 'Rama' nor count the beads on account of a feeling that my end was near. But I was too weak then to turn the wheel. I do count the rosary whenever it helps me in concentrating on Rama. When, however, I rise to a pitch of concentration where the rosary is more a hindrance than a help, I drop it. If it was possible for me to turn the wheel in my bed, and if I felt that it would help me in concentrating my mind on God, I would certainly leave the rosary aside and turn the wheel. If I am strong enough to turn the wheel, and I have to make a choice between counting beads or turning the wheel, I would certainly decide in favour of the wheel, making it my rosary, so long as I found poverty and starvation stalking the land. I do look forward to a time when even repeating the name of Rama will become a hindrance. When I have realized that Rama 'transcends even speech, I shall have no need to repeat the name. The spinning wheel, the rosary and the Ramanama are all the same to me. They subserve the same end, they teach me the religion of service.[7]

In my opinion, God's name and God's work go hand in hand. There is no question of preference because the two are indivisible. A parrot-like repetition of the name is worse than useless, and service or action without the consciousness that it is done in God's name and for God's sake is also valueless, and if we sometimes pass our time in merely repeating the name of the deity as we have to, it is simply a course of preparation for self-dedication, that is, service for the sake of and in the name of God, and when we are thoroughly attuned, continued service in that spirit is itself equal to the repetition of the name of the deity. In the vast majority of cases, however, the setting apart a part of our time for prayer is a vital necessity.[8]

Devotion to duty is itself prayer. We go and pray in order to be qualified for doing actual service. But when one is engaged in actual practice of duty, prayer is merged with the execution of duty. If someone who is engaged in deep prayer, hears the cry of another who is stung by a scorpion, she is bound to leave the prayer and run to help him. Prayer finds fulfilment in the service of the distressed.[9]

Real praying from the heart brings the real work behind it. For in the end work itself becomes prayer.[10]

The real way to pray to Lord Krishna is to do in His name some little service to those who are less fortunate than ourselves.[11]

By not attending prayers in order that they might help in putting out the fire, the women offered real prayers. This is an example of non-action in action. You fulfilled the real purpose of prayers. Moreover, one can go on repeating Ramanama to oneself even while running to the place where fire has started in order to help put it out.

Finally, the person whose life is dedicated to service and who has burnt his or her egotism lives his life in the spirit of prayer. We pray morning and evening in order that we may be able to live thus, and, therefore, when a fire breaks out, or in similar circumstances, one may even drop prayers. But such occasions are rare.[12]

There is no worship purer or more pleasing to God than selfless service of the poor. The rich in their arrogance and intellectual pride often forget God and even question His existence. But God dwells among the poor as they cling to Him as their sole refuge and shelter. To serve the poor is therefore to serve Him.[13]

Q.: Would it not be better for a man to give the time he spends on the worship of God to the service of the poor? And should not true service make devotional worship unnecessary for such a man?

A.: I sense mental laziness as also agnosticism in this question. The biggest of *Karmayogis* never give up devotional song or worship. Idealistically it may be said that true service of others is itself worship and that such devotees do not need to spend any time in songs etc. As a matter of fact, *bhajans* etc. are a help to true service and keep the remembrance of God fresh in the heart of the devotee.[14]

Q.: Are not meditation and worship too sacred a duty?

A.: Meditation and worship are not exclusive things like jewels to be kept locked up in a strong box. They must be seen in every act of ours.[15]

Resign to His Will

A prayer can be offered in connection with some person or thing, and may even be granted. But if it is offered without any such specific end in view, it will confer a greater benefit on the world as well as ourselves. Prayer exerts an influence over ourselves; our soul becomes more vigilant, and the greater its vigilance, the wider the sphere of its influence.

Prayer is a function of the heart. We speak aloud in order to wake it up. The Power that pervades the universe is also present in the human heart. The body does not offer it any obstruction. The obstruction is something of our own making, and is removed by prayer. We can never know if a prayer has or has not yielded the desired result. I may pray for Narmada's relief from pain; even if she is free from pain afterwards, I must not assume that that is due to my prayer.

Prayer is never fruitless, but we cannot know what the fruit of it is. Nor should we imagine that it is a good thing if it yields the desired result. Here too the Gita doctrine has to be practised. We may pray for something and yet remain free from attachment. We may pray for some one's *mukti* (salvation) but should not worry whether he gets or does not get what we want for him. Even if the result is just the opposite of what we had asked for, that is no reason for the conclusion that the prayer has been fruitless.[16]

Commenting on the allegory of Gajendra and Graha, the elephant king and the alligator that adorns the Bhagawata, Gandhiji remarked:

"The moral of the story is that God never fails his devotees in the hour of trial. The condition is that there must be a living faith in and the uttermost reliance on Him. The test of faith is that having done our duty we must be prepared to welcome whatever He may send—joy as well as sorrow, good luck as well as bad.

A man of prayer will in the first place be spared mishaps by the ever merciful Providence but if the mishaps do come he will not bewail his fate but bear it with an undisturbed peace of mind and joyous resignation to His will."[17]

God is the hardest taskmaster I have known on this earth, and He tries you through and through. And when you find that your faith is failing you, and you are sinking, He comes to your assistance somehow or other and proves to you that you must not lose your faith and that He is always at your beck and call, but on His terms, not on your terms. So I have found. I cannot really recall a single instance when at the eleventh hour, He has forsaken me.[18]

How to and Whom to Pray?

"Often, Sir, do you ask us to worship God, to pray but never tell us how to and whom to do so. Will you kindly enlighten me?" asks a reader of *Navajivan*.

Worshipping God is singing the praise of God. Prayer is a confession of one's unworthiness and weakness. God has a thousand names or rather, He is Nameless. We may worship or pray to Him by whichever name that pleases us. Some call Him Rama, some Krishna, others call Him Rahim, and yet others call Him God. All worship the same spirit, but as all foods do not agree with all, all names do not appeal to all. Each chooses the name according to his associations, and He being the In-Dweller, All-Powerful and Omniscient knows our innermost feelings and responds to us according to our deserts.

Worship or prayer, therefore; is not to be performed with the lips, but with the heart. And that is why it can be performed equally by the dumb and the stammerer, by the ignorant and the stupid. And the prayers of those whose tongues are nectared but whose hearts are full of poison are never heard. He, therefore, who would pray to God, must: cleanse his heart. Rama was not only on the lips of Hanuman. He was enthroned in his heart. He gave Hanuman exhaustless strength. In His strength he lifted the mountain and crossed the ocean. It is faith that steers us through stormy seas, faith that moves mountains and faith that jumps across the ocean. That faith is nothing but a living, wide awake consciousness of God within. He who has achieved that faith wants nothing. Bodily diseased he is spiritually healthy, physically pure, he rolls in spiritual riches.

"But how is the heart to be cleansed to this extent?" one might well ask. The language of the lips is easily taught but who can teach the language of the heart? Only the Bhakta- the true devotee-knows it and can teach it. The Gita has defined the Bhakta in three places, and talked of him generally everywhere. But a knowledge of the definition of a Bhakta is hardly a sufficient guide. They are rare on this earth. I have, therefore, suggested the Religion of Service as the means. God of Himself seeks for His seat the heart of him who serves his fellowmen. That is why Narasimha Mehta who "saw and knew" sang, "He is a true Vaishnava who knows to melt at other's woe." Such was Abu Ben Adhem. He served his fellowmen, and therefore, his name topped the list of those who served God.

But who are the suffering and the woe-begone? The suppressed and the poverty-stricken. He who would be a Bhakta; therefore, must serve these by body, soul and mind. How can he who regards the "suppressed" classes as untouchables serve them by the body? He who does not even condescend to exert his body to the extent of spinning for the sake of the poor and trots out lame excuse does not know the meaning of service. An able-bodied wretch deserves no alms, but an appeal to work for his bread. Alms debase him. He who spins before the poor inviting them to do likewise serves God as no one else does. "He who gives Me even a trifle as a fruit or a flower or even a leaf in the spirit of Bhakti is my servant", says the Lord in the Bhagavadgita. As he hath his footstool where live "the humble, the lowliest and lost", spinning, therefore, for such is the greatest prayer, the greatest worship, the greatest sacrifice.

Prayer, therefore, may be done by any name. A prayerful heart is the vehicle and service makes the heart prayerful. Those Hindus who in this age serve the untouchables from a full heart truly pray; the Hindus and those others who spin prayerfully for the poor and the indigent truly pray.[19]

A correspondent writes:

"You say that the rule should be that during prayers, everyone should sit with closed eyes and think of nothing but God. The question arises as to how and in what form we have to think of God?"

True meditation consists in closing the eyes and ears of the mind to all else; except the object of one's devotion. Hence the closing of eyes during prayers is an aid to such concentration. Man's conception of God is naturally limited. Each one has, therefore, to think of Him as best appeals to him, provided that the conception is pure and uplifting.[20]

Prayer brings a peace, a strength and a consolation that

nothing else can give. But it must be offered from the heart. When it is not offered from the heart, it is like the beating of a drum, or just the vocal effect of the throat sounds. When it is offered from the heart, it has the power to melt mountains of misery. Those who want are welcome to try its power.[21]

A person must shed all spiritual dirt at prayer time. As he is ashamed of doing anything immoral while other people are looking on, so should he be in the presence of God. But God knows our every act and every thought. There is not a single moment when we can think any thought or do any act unknown to Him. He who thus prays from the bottom of his heart will in time be filled with the spirit of God and become sinless.[22]

Punctuality at Prayers

It must have been during Bapu's tour of South Bharat in September 1927. The Tamilnad tour had ended, and we were covering Andhra by car. We reached Chikakol at about 10 p.m., and found that the local workers had organized a spinning competition between the best women spinners there, in Bapu's honour. (Chikakol Khadi is famous throughout the length and breadth of Bharat for its remarkable fineness and beauty.) We were dead tired with all the night-and-day travelling in a motor-car, and in no mood for any programmes or competitions. Mahadevbhai and I thought: "Poor Bapu can't get out of this competition, but why shouldn't we? It won't make any difference to anybody whether we go or not. Much better to snatch a little sleep when one can!" So Mahadevbhai and I went off to our sleeping places and fell fast asleep. Bapuji's bed had been prepared for him—we never knew when he came, or how he slept.

We rose at 4 a.m. for prayers. We washed our faces and were just beginning the prayers when Bapu asked: "Did you say your prayers before sleeping last night?" I replied: "I was so tired when I came to bed that I just went off to sleep, clean forgetting my prayers. I remember it just this moment, when you ask us about it."

Mahadevbhai said: "It was the same with me, but just as I was dropping off, I remembered that we had not prayed, so I sat up in bed and rectified the omission. I did not wake Kaka, though."

Then Bapu said, with indescribable pathos: "I sat for an hour or so in the competition, and when I returned, I was so tired that I, too, forgot all about prayer and went to sleep. Then, at about two o'clock, I woke up, and it flashed upon me that I had not said my nightly prayers. I felt such agony that my body was seized with a fit of trembling, and I became all wet with perspiration. I sat up in bed, and was plunged. in a remorse beyond all description. How could I forget Him by whose mercy I live, who strengthens me in all my efforts? How could I forget that Bhagavan? I could not get over my own carelessness. I could not sleep a wink after that. All night I sat up in bed, repenting my mistake and begging His forgiveness."

Saying this he became silent; it may be imagined with what feelings we said our morning prayers that day. Mahadevbhai sang a *bhajan* (hymn). Then Bapu said: "Even while travelling, we must have a fixed time for our evening prayers. We make a mistake in leaving our prayers till we have finished all our work and are preparing to go to bed. From today, we pray punctually at seven o'clock in the evening, no matter where we may happen to be."

We were still journeying by car. Every evening at seven o'clock, we would stop the car, and, whether we were in a forest or in a town, we would say our prayers without fail, at the appointed time.[23]

God's Time Never Stops

It should be the general rule that prayers must not be delayed for anybody on earth. God's time never stops. As a matter of fact, there is no beginning for Him or His time.

...How can anyone afford to miss the time of offering prayers to Him, whose watch never stops?[24]

Forms and Methods of Prayer

I do not like being late for the prayers. Even a minute's delay for the prayer causes me great discomfort.²⁵

Never Miss Prayers

It is five minutes to seven. So you must now be on your way to the prayer-ground. You must keep to whatever time you might fix. I take it that all those who promised to attend prayers are attending them, except for reasons quite beyond their control.²⁶

It is exactly 6.50, so it is time for your morning prayers. You may miss all else but not this. It brings us all together, and all of us together with God. It is a real purifying bath. Just as our body becomes dirty without a bath, so also the pure soul appears impure unless our hearts are cleaned with prayer. Therefore, never miss prayers. You also have an opportunity to meet everyone at the 4 a.m. prayers. It is however, not possible for all ladies to attend that prayer. But at the seven o'clock prayer, they have a chance of getting together. It is possible for all of them to attend it. Mutual contact among Ashram women is very essential.

Give still further thought to the matter of prayers. I also believe that the seven o'clock meeting should not be given up. You have taken it upon yourselves as a special duty to infuse life into these meetings. For the present I can only suggest this. Those of you who have the will and the energy to attend the 4 a.m. prayers may resolve to do so, without entering into any unnecessary discussion about what others might do, and thereafter, continue to keep your resolution, in spite of every hardship, so long as health permits.²⁷

There should be no break in the prayers. Never mind if (they are offered), late. It would be better if it is not late. Even if it is late it should not be that the prayers are not offered (at all). Food can be given up but not the prayers.²⁸

I once saw a beautiful painting in a Roman Catholic Church, the work of a gifted painter. It is the time of prayer. Women have been working in the fields, pick-axes in hand.

As one of them was about to dig with her pick-axe fell from her hand, she bent her body as though kneeling for prayer and started praying. The poet—for the painter is a poet—had imagined the woman as working like a machine. For these women work was worship. There is a saying in Latin which means that bodily labour is a form of worship. Anyone who believes that it is so will automatically kneel down at prayer time. A person who has resolved that he will always get up at four will roll up his bed as the clock strikes four. If such a person misses praying at prayer time, he will feel weary and oppressed and will not be able to concentrate on any work.[29]

I got your letter. One must never forget prayer. As the body craves for food when it is hungry and does not forget about it, so the soul should yearn to pray. The prayer may consist of nothing more than Ramanama, but one ought not to forget it in any circumstances. To the extent that you forget it occasionally, to that extent it is an external thing to you. Prayer must become so intimately part of one's being that at last one's every breath is accompanied by Ramanarna. As an eyelid goes on doing its work, one will go on repeating Rama's name with every breath.[30]

Attendance At Prayers

I hear that attendance at prayers is again becoming thinner. It should not be necessary for me to explain at this hour of the day that no one should expect someone else to stimulate his or her interest in prayers. The interest should be felt within. As the body needs food and feels hungry, so the soul needs and feels hungry for prayer. Prayer is a form of communication with God. So long as 'our need for attendance at prayers is not the same as that for attendance at meals, for which we require no one to goad us, so long our faith in God is weak; or, though we subscribe to the rules of the Ashram we do not observe them and to that extent we are unfaithful to it and violate the vow of truth. Anyone who realizes this will not remain absent at prayers—whether morning or evening—without some strong reason.[31]

If we strive for truth, we would not be content merely to attend prayers but would try to concentrate our attention on them. We would try to follow the songs and the discourses, be punctual in attending the prayers and respond to them as to a fresh experience every day. The freshness does not consist in the variety of *bhajans* or other recitations, but should result from the increasing purity of our heart. We should grow daily more contented and feel greater peace of mind. If we do not have this experience, the fault will lie not with the quality of the prayers but with the element of untruthfulness in us. If we attend the prayers with sincere devotion to truth, we would experience nothing but peace. The faithful who visit temples do not observe the lack of cleanliness in them, or pay attention to the hypocrisy of the priest. They do not see the image as a stone. They experience peace in the midst of noise and return from the temples purified in heart. A person like me who feels suffocated by the noise there and sees the image only as a piece of stone should never visit a temple. God appears to us in the form in which we worship Him. For He is not outside of us. He is in the hearts of us all. If we understand this truth, our simplest and smallest actions would shed luster on us and help us to see God. In order that we may learn this, prayers, spinning, and other daily duties are like a spiritual lighthouse to us or a right angle which is the standard of measurement.[32]

You ought to get up in time and attend prayers every day. You may excuse yourselves from other duties, but never from prayers. You should cultivate such a state of mind that for half an hour you will have only one thought in your mind, and no other. Everyone should set apart some time in this manner for reflection. It provides an opportunity to feel one with all living creatures.[33]

As I have already said, you have come to the Ashram not to lose your Christianity, but to perfect it.

If you don't feel the presence of God at the prayer meetings then remember that the names Rama and Krishna signify the same as Jesus to you.

You should most decidedly not attend these meetings. You should go and pray in your private chamber. The prayer meetings are not meant to force anyone into a position. They are meant for free men and women. The children must attend. Those who abstain from sheer laziness must attend. But for you, no one can misunderstand your abstinence. You will therefore please do that which gives you the greatest peace. The Ashram is nothing if it does not enable you to realize God more and more fully day by day. If on Sundays or any other days you would go to Church of course you shall do so.[34]

The Spiritual Value of Silence

It has often occurred to me that a seeker after truth has to be silent. I know the wonderful efficacy of silence. I visited a Trappist monastery in South Africa. A beautiful place it was. Most of the inmates of that place were under a vow of silence. I inquired of the Father the motive of it and he said the motive is apparent: 'We are frail human beings. We do not know very often what we say. If we want to listen to the still small Voice that is always speaking within us, it will not be heard if we continually speak.' I understood that precious lesson. I know the secret of silence.[35]

Experience has taught me that silence is a part of the spiritual discipline of a votary of truth. Proneness to exaggerate, to suppress or modify the truth, wittingly or unwittingly, is a natural weakness of man, and silence is necessary in order to surmount it. A man of few words will rarely be thoughtless in his speech; he will measure every word. We find so many people impatient to talk. There is no chairman of a meeting who is not pestered with notes for permission to speak. And whenever the permission is given the speaker generally exceeds the time limit, asks for more time, and keeps on talking without permission. All this talking can hardly be said to be of any benefit to the world. It is so much waste of time.[36]

When one comes to think of it one cannot help feeling

that nearly half the misery of the world would disappear if we, fretting mortals, knew the virtue of silence. Before modern civilization came upon us, at least six to eight hours of silence out of twenty-four were vouchsafed to us. Modern civilization has taught us to convert night into day and golden silence into brazen din and noise. What a great thing it would be if we in our busy lives could retire into ourselves each day for at least a couple of hours and prepare our minds to listen in to the Voice of the Great Silence. The Divine Radio is always singing if we could only make ourselves ready to listen to It, but it is impossible to listen in without silence. St. Theresa has used a charming image to sum up the sweet result of silence.

"You will at once feel your senses gather themselves together; they seem like bees which return to the hive and there shut themselves up to work at the making of honey: and this will take place without effort or care on your part. God thus rewards the violence which your soul has been doing to itself; and gives to it such a domination over the senses that a sign is enough when it desires to recollect itself, for them to obey and so gather themselves together. At the first call of the will they come back more and more quickly. At last after many and many exercises of this kind, God disposes them to a state of absolute repose and of perfect contemplation."[37]

Silence is a great help to a seeker after truth like myself. In the attitude of silence the soul finds the path in a clearer light, and what is elusive and deceptive resolves itself into crystal clearness. Our life is a long and arduous quest after Truth, and the soul requires inward restfulness to attain its full height.[38]

The observance of silence is equally important, for through it we pray to the Almighty to keep us always awake to our responsibilities.[39]

Dr. Mott concluded his visit in 1936 with a question on silence. He had done so during a brief flying visit to Ahmedabad in 1928 and during this visit too he asked if Gandhiji had continued to find it necessary in his spiritual quest.

Gandhiji: I can say that I am an everlastingly silent man now. Only a little while ago I have remained completely silent nearly two months and the spell of that silence has not yet broken. I broke it today when you came. Nowadays I go into silence at prayer time every evening and break it for visitors at 2 o'clock. I broke it today when you came. It has now become both a physical and spiritual necessity for me. Originally it was taken to relieve the sense of pressure. Then I wanted time for writing. After, however, I had practised it for some time I saw the spiritual value of it. It suddenly flashed across my mind that that was the time when I could best hold communion with God. And now I feel as though I was naturally built for silence. Of course I may tell you that from my childhood I have been noted for my silence. I was silent at school, and in my London days I was taken for a silent drone by friends.

Dr. Mott: In this connection you put me in mind of two texts from the Bible:

"My soul, be thou silent unto God." "Speak Lord, for Thy servant hearkeneth."[40]

Silent Prayers

As I believe the silent prayer is often mightier than any overt act in my helplessness. I continuously pray in the faith that the prayer of a pure heart never goes unanswered. And, with all the strength at my command, I try to become a pure instrument for acceptable prayer.[41]

I had two aims in practising silent prayer. One was, of course, to give rest to the mind. But it was difficult to turn the mind inward except through such prayer.[42]

My faith is increasing in the efficacy of silent prayer. It is by itself an act—perhaps the highest act, requiring the most refined diligence.[43]

I greatly admire these silent prayers. We must devote a part of our time to such prayers. They afford peace of mind. I have experienced this in my own life. Notwithstanding my manifold activities, I devote as much time as possible to prayer.[44]

A silent prayer is often more effective than the spoken word consciously uttered.[45]

Peace and order are necessary at all gatherings, but are specially so at prayer gatherings. People come together for prayers in order to obtain peace, to hear God's name and to recite it. Therefore, those who come should really attune themselves even at the start from their homes. Let them be silent and let their thoughts dwell as they walk, on prayer. Otherwise coming to prayer was useless.[46]

Silence During Prayers

Five minutes' silence during the evening prayer was suggested by me. It would be better to have the same period of silence in the morning also. If the congregation has its heart in the matter, all sounds must cease by and by. Even the children would learn to co-operate. I have attended meetings where silence was observed for half an hour in England. Silence is looked upon as a very important thing among our people. *Samadhi* means silence. *Muni* (sage) and *mauna* (sagehood, silence) are both derived from the same root. It is true that when we practise silence at first, many thoughts enter our minds and we even begin to doze. Silence is intended to remedy these defects.

We are accustomed to talk much and hear loud sounds. Silence therefore seems difficult. A little practice however enables us to like it, and when we like it it gives us a sense of ineffable peace. We are seekers of truth. We must therefore understand what silence means and observe it accordingly. We can certainly take Ramanama during silence. The fact is that we should prepare the mind for it. We shall realize its value if we bestow a little thought on it.

Can we not sit steadily in the congregation for five minutes? Have you ever been at a dramatic performance? Talking is prohibited in many theatres. Enthusiasts like myself will be there an hour before the play begins. In their enthusiasm they do not mind being silent for that hour. But that is not all. The play takes 4 or 5 hours, during which the spectator has to observe silence. But he likes it all the same. The silence is not burdensome to him because his mind is attuned to it. Why then can we not be silent for 5 minutes for God's sake? If there is a flaw in this argument, do let me know. But if it is sound, keep silence with interest and plead on my behalf with those who are opposed to it.[47]

"True culture requires that there should be perfect peace in the rayer ground at the time of the prayer." There should be an atmosphere of solemnity as in a church, a mosque or a temple. He (Gandhiji) knew that many of the temples were full of clamour. It had hurt him deeply. "We go to the temple to worship not the stone or the metal image but God who resides in it. The image becomes what man makes of it. It has no power independently of the sanctity with which it is invested by the worshipper. Therefore everyone, including children, should observe perfect silence at the time of prayer."[48]

How I Introduced Congregational Prayer

I introduced the practice of having congregational prayer some time before the commencement of the South African Satyagraha struggle. The Indian community there was faced with a grave peril. We did all that was humanly possible. All methods of seeking redress, agitation through the press and the platform, petitions and deputations, were tried out but proved of no avail. What was the Indian community consisting of a mere handful of illiterate indentured labourers mostly, with a sprinkling of free merchants, hawkers etc., to do in the midst of an overwhelming majority of Negroes and Whites? The Whites were fully armed. It was clear that if the Indians were to come into their own, they must forge a weapon which would be different from and infinitely superior to the force which the White settlers commanded in such ample measure. It was then that I introduced congregational prayer in Phoenix and Tolstoy Farm as a means for training in the use of the weapon of Satyagraha or soul force.

The singing of Ramadhun is the most important part of congregational prayer. The millions may find it difficult to correctly recite and understand the Geeta verses and the Arabic and Zend Avesta prayers, but everybody can join in chanting Ramanarna or God's name. It is as simple as it is effective. Only it must proceed from the heart. In its simplicity lies its greatness and the secret of its universality. Anyth;ing that millions can do together becomes charged with a unique power.

I congratulate you on your success in the mass singing of Ramadhun without any previous training. But it is capable of further improvement. You should practise it in your homes. I am here to testify that when it is sung in tune to the accompaniment of *tal*, the triple accord of the voice, the accompaniment and thought creates an atmosphere of ineffable sweetness and strength which no words can describe.[49]

Congregational Prayer

It becomes a man to remember his Maker all the twenty-four hours. If that cannot be done we should at least congregate at prayer time to renew our covenant with God. Whether we are Hindus or Musalmans, Parsis, Christians or Sikhs, we all worship the same God. Congregational prayer is a means for establishing the essential human unity through common worship. Mass singing of Ramadhun and the beating of *tal* are its outward expression. If they are not a mechanical performance but are an echo of the inner unison, as they should be, they generate a power and an atmosphere of sweetness and fragrance which has only to be seen to be realized.[50]

For me it [prayer] has been both a joy , and a privilege, in much as I have felt its elevating influence. I ask you to keep it up. You may not know the verses, you may not know Sanskrit and the hymns, but Ramanama is there for all, the heritage handed down from ages. And I tell you why I ask you to continue this congregational prayer. Man is both an individual and a social being. As an individual he may have his prayer during all the waking hours, but as a member of society he has to join in the congregational prayer. I for one may tell you that when I am alone I do have my prayer, but I do feel very lonely without a congregation to share the prayer with me. I knew and even now know very few of you, but the fact that I had the evening prayers with you was enough for me. Among the many memories that will abide in my heart after I leave Bangalore, not the least will be the prayer meetings. But I shall have my congregation at the next place I reach, and forget the wrench. For one who accepts the brotherhood of man and fatherhood of God, should find a congregation wherever he goes, and he may not hug or nurse the feeling of parting or separation. Please, therefore, keep up the prayer. You can form your own congregation in your own places, and as a last resource one's family can become one's congregation well enough. Do meet every evening at this hour, learn a few hymns, learn the Gita, do the best and the most you can for the purpose of self-purification.[51]

Q. : You believe in mass prayer. Is congregational worship as practised today, a true prayer? In my opinion, it is a degrading thing and therefore dangerous. Jesus said: "When thou prayest, thou shalt not be as the hypocrites are, but enter into thine inner chamber and having shut thy door pray to the Father which is in secret." Most people in a crowd are inattentive and unable to concentrate. Prayer then becomes hypocrisy. The *Yogi* is aware of this. Should not the masses, therefore, be taught self-examination which is the true prayer?

A. : I hold that congregational worship held by me, is true prayer for a collection of men. The convener is a believer and no hypocrite. If he were one, the prayer would be tainted at the source. The men and women who attend do not go to any orthodox prayer from which they might have to gain an earthly end. The bulk of them have no contact with the convener. Hence it is presumed, they do not come for show. They join in because they believe that they somehow or other, acquire merit by having common prayer. That most or some persons are inattentive or unable to concentrate, is very true. That merely shows that they are beginners. Neither inattention nor inability to concentrate are any proof of hypocrisy or falsity. It would be, if they pretended to be attentive when they were not. On the contrary, many have often asked me what they should do, when they are unable to concentrate.

The saying of Jesus quoted in the question, is wholly inapplicable. Jesus was referring to individual prayer and to hypocrisy underlying it. There is nothing in the verse quoted, against collective prayer. I have remarked often enough that without individual prayer, collective prayer is not of much use. I hold that individual prayer is a prelude to collective, as the latter, when it is effective, must lead to the individual. In other words, when a man has got to the stage of heart prayer, he prays always, whether in the secret or in the multitude.

I do not know what the questioner's *Yogi* does or does not. I know that the masses when they are in tune with the Infinite, naturally resort to self-examination. All real prayer must have that end.[52]

Co-operative Prayer

The object of our attending prayers is to commune with God and turn the searchlight inwards so that, with God's help, we can overcome our weaknesses.

I believe that one imbibes pure thought in the company of the pure. Even if there is only one pure man, the rest would be affected by that one man's purity. The condition is that we attend the prayers with that intention, otherwise our coming to the prayers is meaningless.

I go further and maintain that even if we all had our weaknesses but came to the (prayer) meeting with the intention of removing them, our collective effort made from day to day would quicken the progress of reform. For, even as co-operation in the economic or political field is necessary, so is co-operation much more necessary on the moral plane. That is the meaning of the prayer meetings which I have been holding since my return to India.

I, therefore, appeal to you to sit absolutely quiet with your eyes closed, so as to shut yourselves off from outside thoughts for a few minutes at least. This cooperative prayer needs no fasts, no advertisement. It must be free from hypocrisy.[53]

My Faith In Public Prayer

Speaking for myself, I can say that I can do, and have often done, without food for days on end, but I cannot do without prayers even for a single day. Individual prayer is there, but no one should fight shy of collective prayer. Man is a social being. If men and women can eat together, play together and work together, why should they not pray together? Why should anyone feel the need to pray away from everybody's gaze? Is there anything sinful or shameful in prayer that it should not be said in public?

Crowds Attend My Prayers

For close on 50 years, I have been a believer in public prayer. From my earliest days in South Africa, I had among my associates and co-workers men and women of every religion-Hindus, Muslims, Christians and Parsis-who all used to join me in the prayer. In India, men and women in crowds attend my prayers wherever I go. I have been told that one reason why people feel no interest in community prayers may be that they do not come to attend the prayers; they come just to have my *darshan*. Even if it is so they come because they want to join me-a man of prayer.[54]

Individual Prayer

Though I have already written once on this subject, I feel that I should again write something about its importance. It seems to me that they do not realize the necessity of individual prayer. The idea of community prayers arose from the individual's need for prayer. If individuals do not feel such a need, how can a community? Community prayers also are for the benefit of individuals. They help people in their effort to attain knowledge of the self-for self-purification. It is, therefore, necessary that all of us should understand the importance of individual prayer. As soon as a child learns to understand things, its mother ought to teach it to pray. This practice is common to all religions.

There are at least two clear times for such prayer, that is, we should turn our mind to the Lord within immediately on awakening in the morning and when closing our eyes for sleep in the evening. During the rest of the day, every man find woman who is spiritually awake will think of God when doing anything and do that with Him as witness. Such a person will never do anything evil, and a time will come when he or she will think every thought with God as witness and as its Master. This will be a state in which one will have reduced oneself to a cipher. Such a person, who lives constantly in the sight of God, will every moment feel Rama dwelling in his heart.

For such prayers, no special *mantra* or *bhajan* is necessary. Though generally a *mantra* is recited at the commencement and conclusion of every religious act, that is not at all necessary. We have only to turn our thoughts to God, no matter by what name we call Him, by what method and in what condition. Very few form such a habit. If most people followed this practice, there would be less sin and evil in this world and our dealings with one another would be pure. In order that we may attain such a pure state, every body should pray at least at the two times which I have mentioned. Each person may fix other hours, too, according to his convenience, and gradually increase their frequency so that, ultimately his every breath will be accompanied with Ramanama.

Such individual prayer consumes no time at all. It requires not time but wakefulness. As we don't feel that the unceasing action of blinking consumes any time, so also we do not feel that praying inwardly does. But we are aware that the eyelids are doing their work; similarly prayer should go on constantly *in* our heart. Anybody who wishes to pray in this manner should know that he cannot do with an impure heart. He must, therefore, banish all impurity from his heart when praying. As one feels ashamed of doing anything wicked when being observed by somebody, so also should one feel ashamed of acting similarly in the sight of God. But God watches every action and knows every thought of ours. Hence there can be no moment when we can do anything or think any thought unobserved by Him. Thus, anybody who prays to God with his heart will in the end become filled with Him and so become sinless.[55]

I can easily understand your prefering group prayer, for you started praying in that manner. But you must also pray by yourself, even if it be only for one minute. Our aspiration should be that ultimately we shall continually and silently go on repeating God's name in our heart, and that is impossible unless one forms the habit of praying by oneself. One can pray by oneself even while lying in bed, bathing, eating or doing any other work. Thus it can never be a burden. On the contrary, such prayer will lighten one's heart-it ought to do so. If you do not get such experience, then you may know that your prayer is not from the heart.[56]

Individual prayer alone can be the basis of congregational prayer. My emphasis on the latter does not at all mean that I attach greater importance to it. Since we are not used to congregational prayer, I have attempted to show the need for it. What you can experience in seclusion is certainly difficult, if not impossible, to experience in a group. I have also noticed that some people cannot pray except in a group. For such people individual prayer is essential. I would also admit that one can do 'without congregational prayer but certainly not without individual prayer.[57]

Concentration During Prayers

I think I do command concentration, but not well enough to satisfy me. I try earnestly to cultivate such concentration, but I am not impatient.[58]

Q.: Is it possible that during prayers, for thousands who assemble at your prayer gatherings, to concentrate their minds on anything whatever?

A.: I can only answer yes. For, if I did not believe in mass prayer, I should cease to hold public prayers. My experience confirms my belief. Success depends upon the purity of the leader and the faith of the audience. I know instances in which the audience had faith and the leader was an impostor. Such cases will continue to happen. But truth like the sun shines in the midst of the darkness of untruth. The result in my case will be known probably after my death.

Even if your mind wanders when praying, you should keep up the practice. You should retire to a secluded spot, sit in the correct posture and try to keep out all thoughts. Even if they continue to come, you should nevertheless complete the prayer. Gradually the mind will come under control. The Gita also says that the mind is restless, but it tells us that with patient effort we can bring it under control. "We shall never willingly accept defeat, though we lose our life in the struggle."[59]

Compulsory Prayer

Q.: I am a worker in the Rajasthan branch of the A.I.S.A. I believe in prayer but some of my colleagues do not. Still they have got to join in prayer under the rules of the *Sanstha*. They are afraid that, if they refuse, they would lose their job. My view is that the *Sanstha* pays wages to its workers for their eight hours' work. What right has it to insist upon including compulsory participation in prayer by their workers into the bargain.

A. : There can be no such thing as compulsory prayer. A prayer to be prayer must be voluntary. But nowadays people entertain curious ideas about compulsions. Thus, if the rules of your institution require every inmate-paid or unpaid-to attend common prayer, in my opinion you are bound to attend it as you are to attend to your other duties. Your joining the institution was a voluntary act. You knew or ought to have known its rules. Therefore, your attendance at prayer I would regard as a voluntary act, even as I would treat your other work under the contract. If you joined the institution merely because of the wages it offered you should have made it clear to the manager that you could not attend prayer. If in spite of your objection you entered the institution without stating your objection, you did a wrong thing for which you should make expiation. This can be done in two ways-by joining the prayer with your heart in it, or by resigning and paying such compensation as may be necessary for the loss caused by your sudden resignation. Everyone joining an institution owes it to obey the rules framed by the management from time to time. When any new rule is found irksome, it is open to the objector to leave the institution in accordance with the provisions made for resignation. But he may not disobey them whilst he is in it.[60]

The Malady Of Intolerance

The prayer meeting began today as usual. When the verses from the Koran were being recited a member of the audience objected to the recitation. He was arrested by the policeman but Gandhiji immediately stopped the prayer, and requested the policeman who had arrested him to set him free.

He would be ashamed to pray, he said, where a man had been arrested for doing what he had done. He would leave the place, he said only if he were requested to do so by the Mehtars. He would not wait even to consult the trustees as they were after all the trustees of the Mehtars.

Shri G.L. Thatte, General Secretary of the Anti-Pakistan Front was arrested today outside the Valmiki Temple just before Gandhiji came out for the evening prayers.

Earlier in the day Shri Thatte had sent a letter to Gandhiji informing him of his intention to object to the recitation of the verses from the Quran at the prayer.

Another person was arrested a little later when he took

exception to the recitation of Koranic verses during the prayers and shouted *Hindu Dharmaki Jay*. Gandhiji then discontinued the prayers.

Gandhiji requested the police to set the man free as it put him (Gandhiji) to shame if anybody was arrested for objecting to what he did.

Gandhiji deplored such narrow-mindedness on the part of the people. Mere shouting of slogan, would not carry Hinduism anywhere, he said. He was at a loss to understand why some Hindus objected to his reading the Quran verses in his prayer. If at places the Muslims had not behaved as they should, then it did not mean that the Hindus should retaliate by opposing the reading of the Quran.

The verse from the Quran that was being recited, Gandhiji said, was a mighty prayer in praise of God. How did it harm the Hindu religion if the prayer was recited in the Arabic language? He who said so knew neither his religion nor his duty. That prayer could also be recited in a temple.

He had been told by a friend that a prayer with the same meaning was also found in the Yajurveda. Those who had studied the Hindu scriptures knew that among the 108 Upanishads there was one called the Allopanishad. Did not the man who wrote it know his religion? It was said that Guru Nanak himself went to Arabia in search of truth during his religious wanderings.

No religion in the world, Gandhiji continued, could live without self-suffering. A faith gained in strength only when people were willing to lay down their lives for it. The tree of life had to be watered with the blood of martyrs, who had laid down their lives without killing their opponents or intending any harm to them. That was the root of Hinduism and of all other religions.[61]

Fasting and Prayer

Fasting is an institution as old as Adam. It has been resorted to for self-purification or for some ends noble as well as ignoble.

Buddha, Jesus and Mohammed fasted so as to see God face to face. Ramchandra fasted for the sea to give way for his army of monkeys. Parvati fasted to secure Mahadev himself as her Lord and Master. In my fasts I have but followed these great examples, no doubt for ends much less noble than theirs.

* * *

Mere physical capacity to take it is no qualification for it. It is of no use without a living faith in God. It should never be a mechanical effort nor a mere imitation. It must come from the depth of one's soul.[62]

We have it in our Shastras that whenever things go wrong, good people and sages go in for *tapasya*, otherwise known as austerities. Gautama himself, when he saw oppression, injustice and death around him, and when he saw darkness in front of him, at the back of him, and each side of him, went out in the wilderness .and remained there fasting and praying in search of light. And if such penance was necessary for him who was infinitely greater than all of us put together, how much more necessary is it for us?[63]

My religion teaches me that whenever there is distress which one cannot remove, one must fast and pray.[64]

I know now more fully than ever that there is no prayer without fasting, be the latter ever so little. And this fasting relates not merely to the palate, but all the senses and organs. Complete absorption in prayer must mean complete exclusion of physical activities till prayer possesses the whole of our being and we rise superior to, and are completely detached from, all physical functions. That state can only be reached after continual and voluntary crucifixion of the flesh. Thus all fasting, if it is a spiritual act, is an intense prayer or a preparation for it. It is a yearning of the soul to merge in the divine essence.[65]

The prayer is not vain repetition nor fasting mere starvation of the body. Prayer has to come from the heart which knows God by faith, and fasting in abstinence from evil or injurious thought, activity or food. Starvation of the body when the mind thinks of a multiplicity of dishes is worse than useless.[66]

Forms and Methods of Prayer

This is a hoary institution. A genuine fast cleanses body, mind and soul. It crucifies the flesh and to that extent sets the soul free. A sincere prayer can work wonders. It is an intense longing of the soul for its even greater purity. Purity thus gained when it is utilized for a noble purpose becomes a prayer. The mundane use of the *Gayatri*, its repetition for healing the sick, illustrates the meaning we have given to prayer. When the same *Gayatri Japa* is performed with a humble and concentrated mind in an intelligent manner in times of national difficulties and calamities, it becomes a most potent instrument for warding off danger. There can be no greater mistake than to suppose that the recitation of the *Gayatri*, the *namaz* or the Christian prayer are superstitions fit to be practised by the ignorant and the credulous. Fasting and prayer therefore are a most powerful process of purification and that which purifies necessarily enables us the better to do our duty and to attain our goal. If therefore fasting and prayer seem at times not to answer, it is not because there is nothing in them but because the right spirit is not behind them.

A man who fasts and gambles away the whole of the day as do so many on *Janmashtami* day, naturally, not only obtains no result from the fast in the shape of greater purity but such a dissolute fast leaves him on the contrary degraded. A fast to be true must be accompanied by a readiness to receive pure thoughts and determination to resist all Satan's temptations. Similarly, a prayer to be true has to be intelligible and definite. One has to identify oneself with it. Counting beads with the name of Allah on one's lips, whilst the mind wanders in all directions, is worse than useless.[67]

Prayer expresses the soul's longing and fasting sets the soul free for efficacious prayer.

*　*　*

I would urge the modern generation not to regard fasting and prayer with scepticism or distrust. The greatest teachers of the world have derived extraordinary powers for the good of humanity and attained clarity of vision through fasting and prayer. Much of this discipline runs to waste because instead of being matter of the heart, it is often resorted to for stage effect.[68]

It is my conviction and my experience that, if fasting and prayer are done with a sincere heart and in a religious spirit, marvellous results could be obtained from them. There is nothing as purifying as a fast, but fasting without prayer is barren; it may result in a diseased person being restored to health or may only mean a healthy person suffering unnecessarily. A fast undertaken purely for ostentation or to inflict pain on others is an unmitigated sin. Hence, it is only a prayerful fast undertaken by way of penance to produce some effect on oneself which can be called a religious fast. Prayer does not mean begging God for worldly happiness or for the things which advance one's interests; it is the earnest cry of a soul in anguish. It cannot but influence the whole world and cannot but make itself heard in the divine court. When an individual or a nation suffers because of a great calamity, the true awareness of that suffering is prayer; in the presence of this purifying knowledge, physical functions like eating, etc., become less urgent. A mother suffers when her only son dies. She has no desire for eating. A nation is born when all feel the same sort of grief at the suffering of anyone among them; such a nation deserves to be immortal. We are well aware that quite a large number of our brothers and sisters in India live in great suffering and so, truly speaking, we have occasion at every step for prayerful fasting. But our national life has not attained to this degree of intensity and purity. Even so, occasions arise when we suffer acutely.

* * *

The peace and the good that ensue from turning our thoughts to God in a time of sorrow are not to be had in any other way.[69]

The Truest Prayer

Mortification of the flesh has been held all the world over as a condition of spiritual progress. There is no prayer without fasting, taking fasting in its widest sense. A complete fast is a complete and literal denial of self. It is the truest prayer. "Take my life and let it be, always only all for Thee" is not, should not be, a mere lip or figurative expression. It has to be a wreckless and joyous giving without the least reservation. Abstention from food and even water is but the mere beginning, the least part of the surrender.

Whilst I was putting together my thoughts for this article, a pamphlet written by Christians came into my hands wherein was a chapter on the necessity of example rather than precept. In this occurs a quotation from the 3rd chapter of Jonah. The prophet had foretold that Nineveh, the great city, was to be destroyed on the fortieth day of his entering it:

"So the people of Nineveh believed God, and proclaimed a fast, and put on sack-cloth, from the greatest of them even to the least of them. For word came unto the King of Nineveh, and he arose from his throne and he laid his robe from him and covered him with a sack-cloth, and sat in ashes. And he caused it to be proclaimed and published through Nineveh by the decree of the king and the nobles saying, 'Let neither man nor beast, herd nor flock, taste anything; let them not feed, nor drink water. But let man and beast be covered with sack· cloth and cry mightily unto God: yea, let them turn everyone from his evil way, and from the violence that is in their hands. Who can tell if God will turn and repent, and turn away from his fierce anger, that we perish not?' And God saw their works, that they turned from their evil way; and God repented of the evil that he had said that he would do unto them; and he did it not."

Thus this was a "fast unto death". But every fast unto death is not suicide. This fast of the king and the people of Nineveh was a great and humble prayer to God for deliverance. It was to be either deliverance or death. This chapter from the book of Jonah reads like an incident in the Ramayana.[70]

The Shastras tell us that when people in distress prayed to God for relief and He seemed to have hardened His heart, they declared a 'fast unto death' till God had listened to their prayer. Religious history tells us of those who survived their fast, because God listened to them, but it tells us nothing of those who silently and heroically perished in the attempt to win the answer from a deaf God. I am certain that many have died in that heroic manner, but without their faith in God and non-violence being in the slightest degree diminished. God does not always answer prayers in the manner we want Him to. For him life and death are one, and who is able to deny that all that is pure ana good in the world persists because of the silent death of thousands unknown heroes and heroines![71]

I believe that there is no prayer without fasting and there is no real fast without prayer.[72]

The Inner Meaning of the Fast

My religion says that only he who is prepared to suffer can pray to God. Fasting and prayer are common injunctions in my religion. But I know of this sort of penance even in Islam. In the life of the Prophet, I have read that the Prophet often fasted and prayed and forbade others to copy him. Someone asked him why he did not allow others to do the thing he himself was doing. 'Because I live on food divine', he said. He achieved most of his great things by fasting and prayer.

I learnt from him that only he can fast who has inexhaustible faith in God. The Prophet had revelations not in moments of ease and luxurious living. He fasted and prayed, kept awake for nights together and would be on his feet at all hours of the night as he received the revelations. Even at this moment, I see before me the picture of the Prophet thus fasting and praying. It is my own firm belief that the strength of the soul grows in proportion as you subdue the flesh.[73]

Under certain circumstances it (fast) is the one weapon which God has given us for use in times of utter helplessness. We do not know its use or fancy that it begins and ends with mere deprivation of physical food. It is nothing of the kind. Absence of food is an indispensable but not the largest part of it. The largest part is prayer-communion with God. It more than adequately replaces physical food.[74]

It was only when in terms of human effort that I had exhausted all resources and realized my utter helplessness, that I laid my head in God's lap. That is the inner meaning and significance of my fast. You would do well to read and ponder over *Gajendra Moksha* the greatest of devotional poems as I have called it. Then alone perhaps will you be able to appreciate the step I have taken.[75]

The Use of Images in Prayer

I do not forbid the use of images in prayer. I only prefer the worship of the Formless. This preference is perhaps improper. One thing suits one man; another thing will suit another man, and no comparison can fairly be made between the two. You are not right about Shankara and Ramanuja. Spiritual experience has greater influence than environment. The seeker of truth should not be affected by his surroundings but rise above them. Views based on the environment are often found to be wrong. For instance take the case of body and soul. The soul being at present in close contact with the body, we cannot at once realize her as distinct from her physical venture. Therefore it was a very great man indeed who rose above his environment and said, "It (the soul) is not this (the body)." The language of saints like Tukaram should not be taken in a literal sense. I suggest that you read his *abhang, kela maticha pashupati* etc. The moral is that we must realize the idea which underlies the words of holy men. It is quite possible that they worshipped the Formless even while they pictured. God in a particular form. This is impossible for ordinary mortals like ourselves, and therefore we would be in a sorry plight if we did not penetrate a little deeper into the implications of their statements.[76]

Mortal man can only imagine the Unmanifest, the Impersonal, and as his language fails him he often negatively describes It as 'Neti', 'Neti' (Not That, Not That). And so even iconoclasts are at bottom no better than idol-worshippers. To worship a book, to go to a church, or to pray with one's face in a particular direction-all these are forms of worshipping the Formless in an image or idol. And yet both the idol-breaker and the idol-worshipper cannot lose sight of the fact that there is something which is beyond all form, Unthinkable, Formless, Impersonal, Changeless. The highest goal of the devotee is to become one with the object of his devotion. The *bhakta* extinguishes himself and merges into, becomes, *Bhagavan*. This state can best be reached by devoting oneself to some form, and so it is said that the short cut to the Unmanifest is really the longest and the most difficult.[77]

Idol-worship

I do not disbelieve in idol-worship. An idol does not excite any feeling of veneration in me. But I think that idol-worship is part of human nature. We hanker after symbolism. Why should one be more composed in a church than elsewhere? Images are an aid to worship. ...I do not consider idol-worship a sin.[78]

It is being more and more demonstrated that it is the worship of God, be it in the crudest manner possible, which distinguishes man from the brute. It is the possession of that additional quality which gives him such enormous hold upon God's creation. It is wholly irrelevant to show that millions of educated people never enter a church, mosque or temple. Such entry is neither natural nor indispensable for the worship of God. Those even who bow their heads before stocks and stones, who believe in incantations or ghosts, acknowledge a power above and beyond them. It is true that this form of worship is savage, very crude; nevertheless, it is worship of God. Gold is still gold though in its crudest state. It merely awaits refinement to be treated as gold even by the ignorant. No amount of refinement will turn iron ore into gold. Refined worship is doubtless due to the effort of man. Crude worship is as old as Adam, and, as natural to him as eating and drinking, if not more natural. A man may live without eating for days on end, he does not live without worship for a single minute.

He may not acknowledge the fact as many an ignorant man may not acknowledge the possession of lungs or the fact of the circulation of blood.[79]

Idolatry Vs. Idol-worship

Q.: I am a Hindu student. I have been great friends with a Muslim, but we have fallen out over the question of idol-worship. I find solace in idol worship, but I cannot give an answer to my Muslim friend in terms of what may be called convincing. Will 'you say something in *Harijan*?

A. My sympathies are with you and your Muslim friend. I suggest your reading my writings on the question in *Young India* and, if you feel at all satisfied, let your Muslim friend read them too. If your friend has real love for you, he will conquer his prejudice against idol-worship. A friendship which exacts oneness of opinion and conduct is not worth much. Friends have to tolerate one another's ways of life and thought even though they may be different, except where the difference is fundamental. May be your friend has come to think that it is sinful to associate with you as you are an idolater. Idolatry is bad, not so idol-worship. An idolater makes a fetish of his idol. An idol-worshipper sees God even in a stone and therefore takes the help of an idol to establish his union with God. Every Hindu child knows that the stone in the famous temple in Ballaras is not Kashi Vishwanath. But he believes that the Lord of the Universe does reside specially in that stone. This play of the imagination is permissible and healthy. Every edition of the Gita on a book-stall has not that sanctity which I ascribe to my own copy. Logic tells me there is no more sanctity in my own copy than in any other. The sanctity is in my imagination. But that imagination brings about marvellous concrete results. It changes men's lives. I am of opinion that, whether we admit it or not, we axe all idol-worshippers or idolaters, if the distinction I have drawn is not allowed. A book, a building, a picture, a carving are surely all images in which God does reside, but they are not God. He who says they are, errs.[80]

Worship in Temples

Q.: You seem to advocate the starting of temples for Panchamas as a step in the direction of their amelioration. Is it not a fact that the Hindu mind, confined for generations past within things like the 'temple' has generally lost the power of any larger vision of God? When you seek to remove untouchability, when you seek to raise the 'untouchables' and accord them a place of freedom and dignity in society, need you do so by encouraging them to copy the present-day caste Hindus even in the matter of the latter's vices, sins and superstitions? In the course of ameliorating the 'untouchables' may we not also reform the Hindu community as a whole, so far at least as worship of temple gods is concerned? In the course of freeing the depressed classes from their present social disabilities, may we not seek also to free their mind and thought, and thus let social reforms bring into being a broader religious and intellectual outlook?

A. I do not regard the existence of temple all a sin or superstition. Some form of common worship, and a common place of worship appear to be a human necessity. Whether the temples should contain images or not is a matter of temperament and taste. I do not regard a Hindu or a Roman Catholic place of worship containing images as necessarily bad or superstitious and a mosque or a Protestant place of worship being good or free of superstition merely because of their exclusion of images. A symbol such as a Cross or a book may easily become idolatrous, and therefore superstitious. And the worship of the image of child Krishna or Virgin Mary may become ennobling and free of all superstition. It depends upon the attitude of the heart of the worshipper.[81]

Are Temples Necessary?

An American correspondent writes:

"My reading of the history of religion is that every great religious advance has been away from organized and formal religion. The great religious truths which the prophets of religion have apprehended and proclaimed have always been lost when their disciples have tried to localize them in priest craft and temples. Truth is too universal to be confined and made sectarian. Therefore, I consider temples, mosques and churches to be a prostitution of religion. In every nation we have witnessed the degradation of truth and righteousness in the temples; and, in my opinion, in the very conception of organized religion this is certain to follow as a natural consequence. When religion is made a monopoly by the priesthood and temples become vested interests, the great mass of mankind becomes isolated from truth until some new prophets arise who break the bonds of orthodoxy and release the spirits of men from dependence upon the priests and temples.

"Buddha and Jesus, Chaitanya and Kabir realized and taught Truth, which is universal in its character and helpful to all men everyWhere, but the isms which bear their names are exclusive and divisive and, therefore, harmful to those who accept the priestly interpretations of these teachings. Religion loses its human character and deserves its reputation of being called an 'opiate'.

"Therefore, I can see no advantage in gaining permission for the Harijan to enter the temples. I know that justice demands that they shall have the liberty even to do wrong. But if they are to learn the lessons of self-respect which will enable them to take an equal place with caste people in the development of the future of our civilization, I think they must learn an independence of all priests and temples. They must attain a self-realization, which is dependent upon inner rather than outer forces. In the process there is likely to be some extravagance of defiance and bitterness before they actually find themselves. When you spoke in Europe that 'you formerly considered that

God is Truth but now you realized that Truth is God,' you struck a responsive chord in the hearts of all of w, whatever our traditions may have been. But when you become a defender of the faith of temple Hinduism, even though it be a purified type, we feel that you have lost your universal appeal, an appeal which I consider you to have made as a Hindu, but as one of that large body of spiritualminded Hindus who do not look to the temples for the spiritual sustenance of their lives. I do not believe that such men are outside the best traditions of Hinduism but are rather in the line of the creators of the religious spirit which has made the spirituality of India her greatest contribution to humanity.

"Nor do I believe that this higher Hinduism is too high for the Harijans, whose spiritual intuitions have never been dulled by our modem type of education. Buddha, Chaitanya and Kabir all made a large appeal to this class, and the teachings of Jesus were most appreciated, not by the high and mighty, but by publicans and fishermen, who were outside the pale of respectable society. If you were to challenge the untouchables to keep as before 'outside the temples and refuse to accept an inferior status I!) society, by defying the caste leaders, and encourage them to develop their inner resources, I think you would have the support of just as large a community of Hindus as you have in your present programme."

This considered opinion representing a large body of people throughout the world deserves respectful consideration. Such an opinion, however, does not appear before me for the first time. I have had the privilege and opportunity of discussing this subject with many friends in the light it is presented. I can appreciate much of the argument, but I venture to think that it is inconclusive, because it has omitted material facts. Some priests are bad. Temples, churches and mosques very often show corruption, more often deterioration. Nevertheless, it would be impossible to prove that all priests are bad or have been bad and that all churches, temples and mosques are hot-beds of corruption and superstition. Nor does the argument take note of this fundamental fact that no faith has done without a habitation; and I go further that in the very nature of things it cannot exist, so long as man remains as he is constituted. His very body has been rightly called the temple of the Holy Ghost, though innumerable such temples belie the fact and are hot-beds of corruption used for dissoluteness. And I presume that it will be accepted as a conclusive answer to a sweeping suggestion that all bodies should be destroyed for the corruption of many, if it can be shown, as it can be, that there are some bodies which are proper temples of the Holy Ghost. The cause for the corruption of many bodies will have to be sought elsewhere. Temples of stone and mortar are nothing else than a natural extension of these human temples and though they were in their conception undoubtedly habitations of God like human temples, they have been subject to the same law of decay as the latter.

I know of no religion or sect that has done or is doing without its house of God, variously described as a temple, mosque, church, synagogue or *agiari*. Nor is it certain that any of the great reformers including Jesu's destroyed or discarded temples altogether. All of them sought to banish corruption from temples as well as from society. Some of them, if not all, appeared to have preached from temples. I have ceased to visit temples for years, but I do not regard myself on that account as a better person than before. My mother never missed going to the temple, when she was in a fit state to go there. Probably her faith was far greater than mine, though I do not visit temples. There are millions whose faith is sustained through these temples, churches and mosques. They are not all blind followers of a superstition, nor are they fanatics. Superstition and fanaticism are not their monopoly. These vices have their root in our hearts and minds.

My advocacy of temple-entry I hold to be perfectly consistent with the declaration which I often made in Europe that Truth is God. It is that belief which makes it possible, at the risk of losing friendships, popularity and prestige, to advocate temple entry for Harijans. The Truth that I know or I feel I know demands that advocacy from me. Hinduism loses its right to make a universal appeal if it closes its temples to the Harijans.

That temples and temple worship are in need of radical reform must be admitted. But all reform without temple-entry will be to tamper with the disease. I am aware that the American friend's objection is not based upon the corruption or impurity of the temples. His objection is much more radical. He does not believe in them at all. I have endeavoured to show that his position is untenable in the light of facts which can be verified from everyday experience. To reject the necessity of temples is to reject the necessity of God, religion and earthly existence.[82]

Are Places of Worship a Superstition?

A correspondent writes thus passionately:

"I am afraid, there is a little fly in the ointment of your splendid defence (in *Young India* of September 23) of the practice of Divine prayer, especially congregational prayer. At the end of the article, referring to churches, temples and mosques you say, 'these places of worship are not a mere idle superstition to be swept away at the first opportunity. They have survived all attacks up to now and are likely to persist to the end of time.'

"On reading this I asked myself: Attacks by whom? Surely those attacks were not made by atheists or scoffers or humbugs, to anything like the extent to which the opposing sects of God-believers are known to have attacked the places of worship of one another. In fact, most, if not all, of the attacks you speak of were perpetrated by 'godly' zealot *in the name and for the glory of each one's own God.*, It would be insulting your knowledge of world history to cite instances.

"Secondly, I asked myself: Is it true-is it strictly correct to say, that these places of worship have survived all attacks? Again the answer is: Surely not. Witness the site at Kashi (or Banaras) where had stood the temple of Vishwanath for long centuries, since even before Lord Buddha's time—but where now stands dominating the 'Holy City' a mosque built out of

Forms and Methods of Prayer **89**

the ruins of the desecrated old temple by orders of no less a man than the, 'Living Saint' *(Zinda Pir)*, the 'Ascetic King' *(Sulta" Auliva)*, the 'Puritan Emperor'—Aurangazeb. Again, it is not the 'unbelieving' British, but the terrible believer, Ibn Saud, and his Wahabi hosts, that are responsible for the recent demolition and desecration of many places of worship in the Hedjaz (Muslim's 'Holy Land'), over which Musalman Indians are just now so loudly lamenting, and which the Nizam of Hyderabad—alone of all Muslim rulers in the world—has vainly tried to restore with his money.

"Do these facts mean nothing to you, Mahatmaji?"

These facts do mean a great deal to me. They show undoubtedly man's barbarity. But they chasten me. They warn me against becoming intolerant. And they make me tolerant even towards the intolerant. They show man's utter insignificance and thus drive him to pray, if he will not be led to it. For does not history record instances of humbled pride bending the knee before the Almighty, washing His feet with tears of blood and asking to be reduced to dust under His heels? Verily 'the letter killeth, the spirit giveth life'.

The writer who is one of the most regular and painstaking readers of *Young India* should know by this time that places of worship to me are not merely brick and mortar. They are but a shadow of the Reality. Against every church and every mosque and every temple destroyed, hundreds have risen in their places. It is wholly irrelevant to the argument about the necessity of prayer that the so-called believers have belied their belief and that many places renowned for their sacred character have been razed to the ground. I hold it to be enough, and it is enough for my argument, if I can prove that there have been men in the world and there are men today in existence, for whom prayer is positively the bread of life. I recommend to the correspondent the practice of going unobserved to mosques, temples and churches, without any preconceived ideas, and he will discover as I have discovered that there is something in them which appeals to the heart and which transforms those who go there, not for show, not out of shame or fear, but out of simple devotion. It defies analysis. Nevertheless the fact stands that pure-minded people going to the present places of pilgrimage which have become hot-beds of error, superstition, and even immorality, return from them purer for the act of worship. Hence the significant assurance in the Bhagavadgita: 'I make return according to the spirit in which men worship Me'.

What the correspondent has written undoubtedly shows our present limitations which we must try as early as possible to get rid of. It is a plea for purification of religions, broadening of the outlook. That much-needed reform is surely coming. There is a better world consciousness, and may I say that even the reform we all hanker after needs intense prayer in order to achieve deeper purification of self? For without deeper purification of mankind in general, mutual toleration and mutual goodwill are not possible.[83]

Why no Temple in the Ashram?

You did well in writing to me regarding the temple. If you have still something more to say, write to me. I surely don't insist that my view in this matter should prevail. However, my views on this subject are fixed. I have said regarding myself that I am both an image-worshipper and an image-breaker. The God conceived by a human being is bound to be a form, though the image may be only in the mind. In that sense, I am an image-worshipper, But I have never been willing to worship any form or image as God. Towards a form or image, I always feel *neti, uti*. Hence I regard myself as image-breaker. This being my attitude, I have always felt that we should not have any temple in the Ashram. And it was for this reason that we decided to have no building even for prayers. We sit in the open, with the sky above as the root and the horizons in the four sides as the walls. If we wish to maintain an attitude of equality towards all religions, this is how we should live. These days, I am trying to read a little from the Vedas and other sacred books. I see this same thing in them all. There is no mention of image-worship anywhere. But Hinduism has a place for it. We should not, therefore, oppose it. However, image-worship is not obligatory. It is voluntary. I feel, therefore, that it would be better if, as an institution, we kept away from image-worship. If what I have always believed to be a *samadhi* is really a temple, we should not make it a place of public worship. When the owner of the land wished to demolish the structure and carry away the bricks, I paid money to him against the estimated value of the bricks and saved the structure. But I do not wish to turn it into a temple.[84]

Yes, worship of a photograph also is image-worship.

However, there is certainly a difference between meditating on a photograph, on special days and building a temple and installing an image in it. We should not introduce image-worship in the Ashram. The Ashram should have place equally for all religions.[85]

A Model Temple

I mentioned only the other day an ambitious scheme set on foot for a model temple in Rajkot. Several correspondents have taken me to task for advocating temple-entry for Harijans without emphasizing the necessity of temple reform. There is no doubt that temple reform is necessary. But here, again, there is need for caution. Some of them think that it is possible to replace all the existing temples with new ones. I do not share that view. All temples will never be alike. They will always vary, as they have done in the past, with the varying human needs. What a reformer should be concerned with is a radical change more in the inward spirit than in the outward form. If the first is changed, the second will take care of itself. If the first remains unchanged, the second, no matter how radically changed, will be like a whited sepulchre. A mausoleum, however beautiful, is a tomb and not a mosque, and a bare plot of consecrated ground may be a real temple of God.

Therefore the first desideratum is the priest. My ideal

priest must be a man of God. He must be a true servant of the people. He should have the qualifications of a guide, friend and philosopher to those among whom he is officiating. He must be a whole timer with the least possible needs and personal ties. He should be versed in the Shastras. His whole concern will be to look after the welfare of his people. I have not drawn a fanciful picture. It is almost true to life. It is based on the recollections of my childhood. The priest I am recalling was looked up to by the prince and the people. They flocked round him for advice and guidance in the time of their need.

If the sceptics say such a priest is hard to find nowadays, he would be partly right. But I would ask the reformer to wait for building the temple of his ideal till he finds his priest.

Meanwhile let him cultivate in himself the virtues he will have in the priest of his imagination. Let him expect these from the priests of existing temples. In other words, by his gentle and correct conduct, let him infect his immediate surroundings with the need of the times and let him have faith that his thought, surcharged with his own correct conduct, will act more -powerfully than the mightiest dynamo. Let him not be impatient to see the result in a day. A thought may take years of conduct to evolve the requisite power. What are years or generations in the life of a great reform?

Now, perhaps, the reader will follow my view of a model temple. I can present him with no architect's plan and specification. Time is not ripe for it. But that does not baffle the reformer. He can choose the site for his future temple. It must be as extensive as he can get it. It need not be in the heart of a village or a city. It should be easily accessible to the Harijans and the other poor and yet it must not be in an insanitary surroundings. If possible, it should be higher than its surroundings. In any case, I would aim at making the plinth of the actual temple as high as possible. And on this site I should select my plot for daily worship.

Round this will come into being a school, a dispensary, a library, secular and religious. The school may serve also as a meeting or debating hall. I should have a *dharmashala* or guest-house connected with the temple. Each one of these will

Forms and Methods of Prayer

be a separate institution and yet subordinate to the temple and may be built simultaneously or one after another as circumstances and funds may permit. The buildings mayor may not be substantial. If labour is voluntary, as it well may be, with mud and straw a beginning may be made at once. But the temple is not yet built. The foundation was laid when the site was procured, the plot for the temple was selected and the first prayer was offered. For the Bhagavat says, "Wherever people meet and utter His name from their hearts, there God dwells, there is His temple." The building, the deity, the consecration is the province of the priest. When he is found, he will set about his task, but the temple began its existence from the time of the first prayer. And if it was the prayer of true men and women, its continuous progress was assured.

So much for the temple of the future. The reader who cares to study the Rajkot scheme will find that the outward form of my model temple materially corresponds to that in the scheme. Indeed, there is nothing new in my idea or the Rajkot scheme. The village temples of yore had almost all the adjuncts suggested by me.

But we must deal with the existing temples. They can become real Houses of God today, if the worshippers will insist on the priests conforming to the ideal presented by me.[86]

Nature's Temple of Worship

Here in Ceylon where I am writing for *Young India* amid surroundings where nature has bountifully poured her richest treasures, I recall a letter written by a poetically inclined friend from similar scenes. I share with the reader a paragraph from that letter:

"A lovely morning! Cool cloudy, with a drowsy sun whose rays are soft as velvet. It is a strangely quiet morning—there is a hush upon it, as of prayer. And the mists are like incense, and the trees worshippers in a trance, and the birds and insects pilgrims come to chant *bhajans*. Oh! how I wish one could learn true abandonment from Nature! We seem to have forgotten our birth-right to worship where and when and how we please. We build temples and mosques and churches to keep our worship safe from prying eyes and away from outside influences, but we forget that walls have eyes and ears, and the roofs might be swarming with ghosts-who knows!

"Good Gracious, I shall find myself preaching next! How foolish, on a lovely morning like this? A little child in the garden adjoining is singing as unconsciously and joyously as a bird. I feel inclined to go and take the dust of its little feet. And since I cannot pour out my heart in sound as simply as that little one, my only refuge is in silence!"

Churches, mosques and temples, which cover so much hypocrisy and humbug and shut the poorest out of them, seem but a mockery of God and His worship, when one sees the eternally renewed temple of worship under the vast blue canopy inviting every one of us to real worship, instead of abusing His name by quarrelling in the name of religion.[87]

Tree Worship

A correspondent writes:

> "It is a common enough sight in this country to see men and women offering worship to stocks and stones d trees, but I was surprised to find, that even educated women belonging to the families of enthusiastic social workers were not above this practice. Some of these sisters and friends defend the practice by saying, that since it is founded on pure reverence for the divine in nature and no false beliefs, it cannot be classed as superstition, and they cite the name of Satyavan and Savitri whose memory, they say, they commemorate in that way. The argument does not convince me. May I request you to throw some light on the matte."

I like this question. It raises the old, old question of image-worship. I am both a supporter and opponent of image-worship. When image-worship degenerates into idolatry and becomes encrusted with false beliefs and doctrines, it becomes a necessity to combat it as a gross social evil. On the other hand image-worship in the sense of investing one's ideal with a concrete shape is inherent in man's nature, and even valuable as an aid to devotion.

Thus we worship an image when we offer homage to a book which we regard as holy or sacred. We worship an image when we visit a temple or a mosque with a feeling of sanctity or reverence. Nor do I see any harm in all this. On the contrary endowed as man is with a finite, limited understanding, he can hardly do otherwise.

Even so far from seeing anything inherently evil or harmful in tree worship, I find in it a thing instinct with a deep pathos and poetic beauty. It symbolizes true reverence for the entire vegetable kingdom, which with its endless panorama of beautiful shapes and forms, declares to us as it were with a million tongues the greatness and glory of God. Without vegetation our planet would not be able to support life even for a moment. In such a country especially, therefore, in which there is a scarcity of trees, tree worship assumes a profound economic significance.

I, therefore, see no necessity for leading a crusade against tree worship. It is true, that the poor simple-minded women who offer worship to trees have no reasoned understanding of the implications of their act. Possibly they would not be able to give any explanation as to why they perform it. They act in the purity and utter simplicity of their faith. Such faith is not a thing to be despised; it is a great and powerful force that we should treasure.

Far different, however, is the case of vows and prayers which votaries offer before trees. The offering of vows and prayers for selfish ends, whether offered in churches, mosques, temples or before trees and shrines, is a thing not to be encouraged. Making of selfish requests or offering of vows is not related to image-worship as effect and cause. A personal selfish prayer is bad whether made before an image or an unseen God.

Let no one, however, from this understand me to mean, that I advocate tree worship in general. I do not defend tree worship because I consider it to be a necessary aid to devotion, but only because I recognize, that God manifests Himself in innumerable forms in this universe, and every such manifestation commands my spontaneous reverence.[88]

Atmosphere for Prayers

My prayers here (first-class on a ship) lack the depth, the serenity and concentration they had when I was in gaol.

I am not writing all this in a frivolous mood, but after deep reflection. I think of these things everyday. . .. I have realized that those who wish to serve God cannot afford to pamper themselves or to run after luxury. Prayers do not come easily in an atmosphere of luxuries. Even if we do not ourselves share the luxuries, we cannot escape their natural influence. The energy that we spend in resisting that influence is at the cost of our devotional efforts.[89]

The Place of Prayer in Ashram Life

I

If insistence on truth constitutes the root of the Ashram, prayer is the principal feeder of that root. The social (as distinguished from the individual) activities of the Ashram commence everyday with the congregational morning worship at 4-15 to 4-45 a.m. and close with the evening prayer at 7 to 7-30 p.m. Ever since the Ashram was founded, not a single day has passed to my knowledge without this worship. I know of several occasions when owing to the rains only one responsible person was present on the prayer ground.

All inmates are expected to attend the worship except in the case of illness or similar compelling reason for absence.

Forms and Methods of Prayer

This expectation has been fairly well fulfilled at the evening prayer, but not in the morning.

The time for morning worship was as a matter of experiment fixed at 4, 5, 6 and 7 a. m., one after another. But on account of my persistently strong attitude on the subject, it has been fixed at last at 4-20 a.m. With the first bell at 4 everyone rises from bed and after a wash reaches the prayer ground by 4-20.

I believe that in a country like India the sooner a man rises from bed the better. Indeed millions must necessarily rise early. If the peasant is a late riser, his crops will suffer damage. Cattle are attended to and cows are milked early in the morning. Such being the case, seekers of saving truth, servants of the people or monks may well be up at 2 or 3; it would be surprising if they are not. In all countries of the world devotees of God and tillers of the soil rise early. Devotees take the name of God and peasants work in their fields serving the world as well as themselves. To my mind both are worshippers. Devotees are deliberately such while cultivators by their industry worship God unawares, as it helps to sustain the world. If instead of working in the fields, they took to religious meditation, they would be failing in their duty and involving themselves and the world in ruin.

We may or may not look upon the cultivator as a devotee, but where peasants, labourers and other people have willy-nilly to rise early, how can a worshipper of Truth or servant of the people be a late riser? Again in the Ashram we are trying to co-ordinate work and worship. Therefore I am definitely of opinion that all able-bodied people in the Ashram must rise early even at the cost of inconvenience. 4 a.m. is not early but the latest time when we must be up and doing.

Then again we have to take a decision on certain questions. Where should the prayers be offered? Should we erect a temple or meet in the open air? Then again, should we raise a platform or sit in the sands or the dust? Should there be any images? At last we decided to sit on the sands under the canopy of the sky and not to install any image. Poverty is an Ashram observance. The Ashram exists in order to serve the starving millions. The poor have a place in it no less than others. It receives with open arms all who are willing to keep the rules. In such an institution, the house of worship cannot be built with bricks and mortar, the sky must suffice for roof and the quarters for walls and pillars. A platform was planned but discarded later on, as its size would depend upon the indeterminate number of worshippers. And a big one would cost a large sum of money. Experience has shown the soundness of the decision not to build a house or even a platform. People from outside also attend the Ashram prayers, so that at times the multitude present cannot be accommodated on the biggest of platforms.

Again as the Ashram prayers are being increasingly imitated elsewhere, the sky-roofed temple has proved its utility. Morning and evening prayers are held wherever I go. Then there is such large attendance, especially in the evening, that prayers are possible only on open grounds. And if I had been in the habit of worshipping in a prayer-hall only, I might perhaps never have thought of public prayers during my tours.

Then again all religions are accorded equal respect in the Ashram. Followers of all faiths are welcome there; they may or may not believe in the worship of images. No image is kept at the congregational worship of the Ashram in order to avoid hurting anybody's feelings. But if an Ashramite wishes to keep an image in his room he is free to do so.

II

At the morning prayer we first recite the *shlokas* (verses) printed in *Ashram Bhajanuvali* (hymnal), and then sing one *bhajan* (hymn) followed by Ramadhun (repetition of Ramanama) and Gitapath (recitation of the Gita). In the evening we have recitation of the last 19 verses of the second chapter of the Gita, one *bhajan* and Ramadhun and then read some portion of a sacred book.

The *shlokas* were selected by Shri Kaka Kalelkar who has been in the Ashram since its foundation. Shri Maganlal Gandhi met him in Santiniketan, when he and the children of the Phoenix Settlement went there from South Africa while I was still in England. Dinabandhu Andrew and the late Mr. Pearson were then in Santiniketan. I had advised Maganlal to stay at some place selected by Andrews. And Andrews selected Santiniketan for the party. Kaka. was a teacher there and came into close contact with Maganlal. Maganlal had been feeling the want of a Sanskrit teacher which was supplied by Kaka. Chintamani Shastri assisted him in the work. Kaka taught the children how to recite the verses repeated in prayer. Some of these verses were omitted in the Ashram prayer in order to save time. Such is the history of the verses recited at the morning prayer all these days.

The recitation of these verses has often been objected to on the ground of saving time or because it appeared to some people that they could not well be recited by a worshipper of truth or by a non-Hindu. There is no doubt that these verses are recited only in Hindu society, but I cannot see why a non-Hindu may not join in or be present at the recitation. Muslim and Christian friends who have heard the verses have not raised any objection. Indeed they need not cause annoyance to any one who respects other faiths as much as he respects his own. They do not contain any reflection on other people. Hindu being in an overwhelming majority in the Ashram, the verses must be selected from the sacred books of the Hindus. Not that nothing is sung or recited from non-Hindu scriptures. Indeed there were occasions on which Imamsaheb recited verses from the Quran. Muslim and Christian hymns are often sung.

But the verses were strongly attacked from the standpoint of truth. An Ashramite modestly but firmly argued that the worship of Sarasvati, Ganesh and the like was violence done to truth; for no such divinities really existed as Sarasvati seated on a lotus with a *vina* (kind of musical instrument) in her hands, or as Ganesh with a big belly and an elephant's trunk. To this argument I replied as follows:

"I claim to be a votary of truth, and yet I do not mind reciting these verses or teaching them to the children. If we condemn some *shlokas* on the strength of this argument, it would be tantamount to an attack on the very basis of Hinduism. Not that we may not condemn anything in Hinduism which is fit for condemnation, no matter how ancient it is. But I do not believe that this is a weak or vulnerable point of Hinduism. On the other hand I hold that it is perhaps characteristic of our faith. Sarasvati and Ganesh are not independent entities. They are all descriptive names of one God. Devoted poets have given a local habitation and a name to His countless attributes. They have done nothing wrong. Such verses deceive neither the worshippers nor others. When a human being praises God he imagines Him to be much as he thinks fit. The God of his imagination is there for him. Even when we pray to a God devoid of form and attributes, we do in fact endow Him with attributes. And attributes too are form. Fundamentally God is indescribable in words. We mortals must of necessity depend upon the imagination which makes and sometimes mars us too. The qualities we attribute to God with the purest of motives are true for us but fundamentally false, because all attempts at describing Him must be unsuccessful. I am intellectually conscious of this and still I cannot help dwelling upon the attributes of God. My intellect can exercise no influence over my heart. I am prepared to admit that my heart in its weakness hankers 'after a God with attributes. The *shlokas* which I have been reciting every day for 'the last fifteen years give me peace and hold good for me. In them I find beauty as well as poetry. Learned men tell many stories about Sarasvati, Ganesh and the like, which have their own use. I do not know their deeper meaning, as I have not gone into it, finding it unnecessary for me. It may be that my ignorance is my salvation. I did not see that I needed to go deep into this as a part of my quest of truth. It is enough that I know my God, and although I have still to realize His living presence, I am on the right path to my destination."

I could hardly expect that the objectors should be satisfied with this reply. An *ad hoc* committee examined the whole question fully and finally recommended that the *shlokas* should remain as they were, for every possible selection would be viewed with disfavour by some one or other.

III

A hymn was sung after the *shlokas*. Indeed singing hymns was the only item of the prayers in South Africa. The *shlokas* were added in India. Maganlal Gandhi was our leader in song. But we felt that the arrangement was unsatisfactory. We should have an expert singer for the purpose, and that singer should be one who would observe the Ashram rules. One such was found in Narayan Moreshvar Khare, a pupil of Pandit Vishnu Digambar, whom the master kindly sent to the Ashram. Pandit Khare gave us full satisfaction and is now a full member of the Ashram. He made hymn-singing interesting, and the *Ashram Bhajanavali* (hymnal) which is now read by thousands was in the main compiled by him. He introduced Ramadhun, the third item of our prayers.

The fourth item is recitation of verses from the Gita. The Gita has for years been an authoritative guide to belief and conduct for the Satyagraha Ashram. It has provided us with a test with which to determine the correctness or otherwise of ideas and courses of conduct in question. Therefore we wished that all Ashramites should understand the meaning of the Gita and if possible commit it to memory. If this last was not possible, we wished that they should at least read the original Sanskrit with correct pronunciation. With this end in view we began to recite part of the Gita everyday. We would recite a few verses everyday and continue the recitation until we had learnt them by heart. From this we proceeded to the *parayan*. And the recitation is now so arranged that the whole of the Gita is finished in fourteen days, and everybody knows what verses will be recited on any particular day. The first chapter is recited on every alternate Friday, and we shall come to it on Friday next (June 10, 1932). The seventh and eighth, the twelfth and thirteenth, the fourteenth and fifteenth, and the sixteenth and seventeenth chapters are recited on the same day in order to finish 18 chapters in 14 days.

At the evening prayer we recite the last 19 verses of the second chapter of the Gita as well as sing a hymn and repeat Ramanama. These verses describe the characteristics of the *sthitaprajna* (the man of stable understanding), which a Satyagrahi too must acquire, and are recited in order that he may constantly bear them in mind.

Repeating the same thing at prayer from day to day is objected to on the ground that it thus becomes mechanical and tends to be ineffective. It is true that the prayer becomes mechanical. We ourselves are machines, and if we believe God to be our mover, we must behave like machines in His hands. If the sun and other heavenly bodies did not work like machines, the universe would come to a standstill. But in behaving like machines, we must not behave like inert matter. We are intelligent beings and must observe rules as such.

The point is not whether the contents of the prayer are always the same or differ from day to day. Even if they are full of variety, it is possible that they will become ineffective. The Gayatri verse among Hindus, the confession of faith *(kalma)* among Mussalmans, the typical Christian prayer in the Sermon on the Mount have been recited by millions for centuries everyday; and yet their power has not diminished but is ever on the increase. It all depends upon the spirit behind the recitation. If an unbeliever or a parrot repeats these potent words, they will fall quite flat. On the other hand when a believer utters them always, their influence grows from day to day.

Our staple food is the same. The wheat-eater will take other things besides wheat, and these additional things may differ from time to time, but the wheat bread will always be there on the dining table. It is the eater's staff of life, and he will never weary of it. If he conceives a dislike for it, that is a sign of the approaching dissolution of his body.

The same is the case with prayer. Its principal contents must be always the same. If the soul hungers after them. she will not quarrel with the monotony of the prayer but will derive nourishment from it. She will have a sense of deprivation on the day that it has not been possible to offer prayer. She will be more downcast than one who observes a physical fast. Giving up food may now and then be beneficial for the body; indigestion of prayer for the soul is something never heard of.

The fact is that many of us offer prayer without our soul being hungry for it. It is a fashion to believe that there is a soul; so we believe that she exists. Such is the sorry plight of many among us. Some are intellectually convinced that there is a soul, but they have not grasped that truth with the heart; therefore they do not feel the need for prayer. Many offer prayer because they live in society and think they must participate in its activities. No wonder they hanker after variety. As a matter of fact however they do not *attend* prayer. They want to enjoy the music or are merely curious or wish to listen to the sermon. They are not there to be one with God.

IV

Prarthana (Gujarati word for prayer) literally means to ask for something, that is, to ask God for something in a spirit of humility. Here it is not used in that sense, but in the sense of praising or worshipping God, meditation and self-purification.

But who is God? God is not some person outside ourselves or away from the universe. He pervades every thing, and is omniscient as well as omnipotent. He does not need any praise or petitions. Being immanent in all beings, He hears very thing and reads our innermost thoughts. He abides in our hearts and is nearer to us than the nails are to the fingers. What is the use of telling Him anything?

It is in vie of this difficulty that *Prarthana* is further paraphrased as self-purification. When we speak out aloud at prayer time, our speech is addressed not to God but to ourselve, and is intended to shake off our torpor. Some of us are intellectually aware of God, while others are afflicted by doubt. None has been Him face to face. We desire to recognize and realiz Him, to become one with Him, and seek to gratify that desire through prayer.

This God whom we seek to realize is Truth. Or to put it in another way Truth is God. This Truth is not merely the truth we are expected to speak. It is That which alone is, which constitutes the stuff of which all things are made, which subsists by virtue of its own power, which is not supported by anything else but supports everything that exists. Truth alone is eternal, everything else is momentary. It need not assume shape or form. It is pure intelligence as well as pure bliss. We call it Ishvara because everything is. regulated by Its 'will.

It and the law it promulgates are one. Therefore it is not a blind law. It governs the entire universe.

To propitiate this Truth, is *Prarthana* which in effect means an earnest desire to be filled with the spirit of Truth. This desire should be present all the twenty-four hours. But our souls are too dull to have this awareness day and night. Therefore we offer prayers for a short time in the hope that a time will come when all our conduct will be one continuously sustained prayer.

Such is the ideal of prayer for the Ashram, which at present is far, far away from it. The detailed programme outlined above is something external, but the idea is to make our very hearts prayerful. If the Ashram prayers are not still attractive, if even the inmates of the Ashram attend them under compulsion of a sort, it only means that none of us is still a man of prayer in the real sense of the term.

In heartfelt prayer the worshipper's attention is concentrated on the object of worship so much so that he is not conscious of anything else besides. The worshipper has well been compared to a lover. The lover forgets the whole world and even himself in the presence of the beloved. The identification of the worshipper with God should be closer still. It comes only 'after much striving, self-suffering *(tapas)* and self-discipline. In a place which such a worshipper sanctifies by his presence, no inducements need be offered to people for attending prayers, as they are drawn to the house of prayer by the force of his devotion.

We have dealt so far with congregational prayer, but great stress is also laid in the Ashram on individual and solitary prayer. One who never prays by himself may attend congregational prayers but will not derive much advantage from them. They are absolutely necessary for a congregation, but as a congregation is made up of individuals, they are fruitless without individual prayers. Every member of the Ashram is therefore reminded now and then that he should of his own accord give himself up to self-introspection at all times of the day. No watch can be kept that he does this, and no account can be maintained of such silent prayer. I cannot say how far it prevails in the Ashram, but I believe that some are making more or less effort in that direction.[90]

The Ashram Prayer

I

The Ashram prayer has become very popular. Its development has been spontaneous. The *Ashram Bhajanavali* (Hymn Book) has gone into several editions and is increasingly in demand. The birth and growth of this prayer has not been artificial. There is a history attached to almost every *shloka* and every selected *bhajan*. The *Bhajanavali* contains among others *bhajans* from Muslim Sufis and Fakirs, from Guru Nanak, and from the Christian hymnary. Every religion seems to have found a natural setting in the prayer book.

Chinese, Burmese, Jews, Ceylonese, Muslims, Parsis, Europeans and Americans have all lived in the Ashram from time to time. In the same way two Japanese Sadhus came to me in Maganwadi in 1935. One of them was with me till the other day when war broke out with Japan. He was an ideal inmate of our home in Sevagram. He took part in every activity with zest. I never heard of his quarrelling with anyone. He was a silent worker. He learnt as much Hindi as he could. He was a strict observer of his vows. Every morning and evening he could be seen going round with his drum and heard chanting his *mantra*. The evening worship always commenced with his *mantra* नम्यो हो रेंगे क्यों which means "I bow to the Buddha, the giver of true religion". I shall never forget the quickness, the orderliness and utter detachment with which he prepared himself the day the police came without notice to take him away from the Ashram. He took leave of me after, reciting his favourite *mantra* and left his drum with me. "You are leaving us, but your *mantra* will remain an integral part of our Ashram prayer," were the words that came spontaneously to my lips. Since then, in spite of his absence, our morning and evening worship has commenced with the *mantra*. For me it is a constant reminder of Sadhu Keshav's purity and single-eyed devotion. Indeed its efficacy lies in that sacred memory.

While Sadhu Keshav was still with us Bibi Raihana Tyabji also came to stay at Sevagram for a few days. I knew her to be a devout Muslim but was not aware, before the death of her illustrious father, of how wellversed she was in Quran Sharif. When that jewel of Gujarat, Tyabji Saheb, expired, no sound of weeping broke the awful silence in his room. The latter echoed with Bibi Raihana's sonorous recitation of verses from the Quran. Such as Abbas Tyabji Saheb cannot die. He is ever alive in the example of national service which he has left behind. Bibi Raihana is an accomplished singer with an ample repertory of *bhajans* of all kinds. She used to sing daily as well as recite beautiful verses from the Quran. I asked her to teach some verses to any of the inmates who could learn them, and she gladly did so. Like so many who come here she had become one of us. Raihana went away when her visit was over, but she has left a fragrant reminder of herself. The well-known 'al Ikhlas and al Fateh' have been included in the Ashram worship. The following is a translation of it:

"1. I take refuge in Allah from Satan the accursed.

"2. Say: He is God, the one and only God,
 the Eternal, Absolute,
He begetteth not nor is He begotten,
And there is none like unto Him.

"3. Praise be to God
The Cherisher and Sustainer of the worlds,
Most Gracious, most Merciful,
Master of the Day of Judgment,
Thee do we worship
And thine aid we seek.
Show us the straight way,
The way of those on whom
Thou hast bestowed Thy Grace,
Those whose (portion) is not wrath
And who go not astray."

I am writing this note in reply to an ardent Hindu friend who thus gently reproached me: "You have now given the *Kalma* a place in the Ashram. What further remains to be done to kill your Hinduism?"

I am confident that my Hinduism and that of the other Ashram Hindus has grown thereby. There should be in us an equal reverence for all religions. Badshah Khan, whenever he comes, joins in the worship here with delight. He loves the tune to which the Ramayana is sung, and he listens intently to the Gita. His faith in Islam has not lessened thereby. Then why may I not listen to the Quran with equal reverence and adoration in my heart?

Vinoba and Pyarelal studied Arabic and learnt the Quran in jail. Their Hinduism has been enriched by this study. I believe that Hindu-Muslim unity will come only through such spontaneous mingling of hearts and no other. Rama is not known by only a thousand names. His names are innumerable and He is the same whether we call him Allah, Khuda, Rahim, Razzak, the Breadgiver, or any name that comes from the heart of a true devotee.[91]

During the three days I passed in Shrinagar though I had prayers in the compound of Lala Kishorilal's bungalow, where I was accommodated, I made no speeches. I had so declared before leaving Delhi. But some of the audience sent me questions. One was:

I attended your prayer meeting last evening in which you recited two prayers of the other communities. May I know what is your idea in doing so and what you mean by a religion?"

As I have observed before now, the selection from the Quran was introduced some years ago on the suggestion of Raihana Tyabji who was then living in the Sevagram Ashram and the one from the Parsi prayers at the instance of Dr. Gilder who recited the Parsi prayer on the break of my fast in the Aga Khan Palace during our detention. I am of opinion that the addition enriched the prayer. It reached the hearts of a larger audience than before. It certainly showed Hinduism in its broad and tolerant aspect. The questioner ought also to have asked why the prayer commenced with the Buddhist prayer in Japanese. The selections of the stanzas of the prayer has a history behind it befitting the sacred character. The Buddhist prayer was the prayer with which the whole of Sevagram resounded in the early morning when a good Japanese monk was staying at the Sevagram Ashram and who by his silent and dignified conduct had endeared himself to the inmates of the Ashram.[92]

About Prayer at the Ashram

What you say about prayer at the Ashram is largely true. It is still a formal thing, soulless; but I continue it in the hope of it becoming a soulful thing. Human nature is much the same whether in the East or in the West. It does not therefore surprise me that you have not found anything special about prayers in the East and probably the Ashram prayer is a hotchpot of something Eastern and something Western. As I have no prejudice against taking anything good from the West or against giving up anything bad in the East, there is an unconscious blending of the two. For a congregational life a congregational prayer is a necessity and, therefore, form also is necessary. It need not be considered on that account to be hypocritical or harmful. If the leader at such congregational prayer meetings is a good man the general level of the meeting is also good. The spiritual effect of an honest intelligent attendance at such congregational prayers is undoubtedly great. Congregational prayer is not intended to supplant individual prayer, which, as you well put it, must be heartfelt and never formal. It is there you are in tune with the Infinite. Congregational prayer is an aid to being in tune with the Infinite. For man who is a social being cannot find God unless he discharges social obligations and the obligation of coming to a common prayer meeting is perhaps the supremest. It is a cleansing process for the whole congregation. But, like all human institutions, if one does not take care, such meetings do become formal and even hypocritical. One has to devise methods of avoiding the formality and hypocrisy. In all, especially in spiritual matters, it is the personal equation that counts in the end.

The roll call is not the ordinary roll call. It is a note of the results of the daily *yajna*, that is, sacrifice. Everyone says that he has spun. Spinning has been conceived in a sacrificial spirit. The idea is to see God through service of the millions. The day must not close without every member of the congregation confessing whether he or she has or has not performed the daily sacrifice to the measure of his or her promise. It is therefore not business at the end of the prayer, but it is the finishing touch to the prayer. It is not done at the beginning of the meeting, because those who are late should have the opportunity of registering their sacrifice. Remember, too, this is a sacrifice not intended to be made in secret. It is designed to be done in the open.[93]

If the children take no interest in any of the prayers, a special item can be included for them, as used to be done by Prabhudas. I should be happy if they sit through the prayers with faith and in stillness.

I did not say it by way of praise that the same prayers have continued for sixteen years. It was only a statement of fact. I did not wish to suggest that all have been attending the prayers for so many years. The Ashram has clung to these prayers in the face of all troubles and criticisms and quite a few people have derived peace of mind from them. All that I intended to say was that these prayers ought not to be given up or altered without a strong reason.[94]

During prayers at the Ashram, none should start reciting or singing before the leader begins. And again, the rule is that when he leads, only those can join in the recitation or singing who can do so in tune. When the whole community sings harmoniously in one tune, their singing never fails to produce an effect. Nor does silence fail. Both are beneficial, each in its proper place. In offering oblations, etc., at a sacrifice, the incantations used to be chanted aloud in the belief that thousands were witnessing the ceremony with reverence. Once that became a custom, even when only five or ten persons are present the incantations at a sacrifice continue to be chanted aloud.[95]

Prayer is the very foundation of the Ashram. We should, therefore, clearly understand what it means. If it is not offered from the heart, it is no prayer at all. We rarely see anybody dozing while eating. Prayer is a million times more important than food. If anybody dozes at prayer time, his condition must be pitiable indeed. If we miss the prayer, we should feel deeply pained. We should not mind if we miss a meal, but we should never miss a prayer. Missing a meal is sometimes beneficial for health. Omitting prayer never is.

If any person dozes at the time of prayer, feels lazy or talks with his neighbours while the prayer is going on, does not fix his attention on it and lets his thoughts wander, he has as good as absented himself from it. His physical presence is mere show. He is, therefore, doubly guilty; he has absented himself from the prayer and has deceived the people. To deceive means to act untruthfully, and, therefore, to violate the vow of truth.

If, however, anybody feels sleepy or bored against his will, what should he do? But this can never happen. If we run straight from the bed to the prayer meeting, we are bound to feel sleepy. Before going to the meeting, we should rouse ourselves fully and brush our teeth, and resolve to remain awake and alert. In the meeting we should not sit close to one another, should sit erect like a walking-stick, breathe slowly and, if we can speak the words correctly, join in reciting the verses or singing the *bhajans*, silently to ourselves if not loudly, If we cannot do even this, we may go on repeating Ramanama. If we still cannot control our body, we should keep standing. No one, whether a grown-up person or a child, should feel shame in doing so. Gorwn-up persons should occasionally keep standing, even if they do not feel sleepy, in order to create an atmosphere in which nobody would feel ashamed of standing.

Everyone should make an effort and understand as soon as possible the meaning of what is recited or sung for prayer. Even if a person does not know Sanskrit, he should learn the meaning of each verse and meditate over it.[96]

Time Taken Up By Prayers

We must not grudge it. Islam enjoins 5 prayers a day each of which would take at least 15 minutes, and at which the same verses have to be repeated. Christian prayers contain one permanent item which also takes 15 minutes each time. In churches belonging to the Catholics and to the Established Church in England devotions take at least half an hour in the morning, at noon and again in the evening. This is not too much for the devotee. Finally, none of us has now the right to modify the order of the various items in our prayers. The subject has been thoroughly discussed already, and the discussion closed. We have to learn to appreciate our prayers and make them an instrument of the beatific vision. We must derive our daily spiritual nutrition from them. Let us not think of changes but pour our whole soul into them, such as they are.[97]

Prayers have often been attacked, but they have been kept up for 16 years. How much time do they take? How much of the time can be saved? Anyone who accepts the necessity of prayers will not grudge the time given to them.[98]

Prayers Especially for Women
From Manibehn's Notes

The first three verses which were always recited at the morning prayers for women contain the moving appeal of Draupadi to Shri Krishna when Duryodhan attempted to pull off her clothes in the court of the Kauravas.

The verses are:

गोविन्द, द्वारिकावासिनः, कृष्ण, गोपीजनप्रिय ।
कौरवैः परिभूतां मां किं न जानासि केशव ॥
हे नाथ, हे रमानाथ, ब्रजनाथार्तिनाशन ।
कौरवार्णवमग्नां मां युद्धस्व जनार्दन ॥
कृष्ण, कृष्ण, महायोगिन्, विश्वात्मन् विश्वभावन ।
प्रपन्नां पाहि गोविन्द, कुरुमध्येऽवसीदतीम् ॥

* * *

Draupadi showed as much strength as Yudhishthir did. Draupadi had five husbands at one time and yet has been called 'chaste' *(sati)*. This is because in that age, just as a man could marry several wives, a woman (in certain regions) could marry several husbands. The mores about marriage change with time and place.

From another point of view, Draupadi can be regarded to symbolise the human mind or intelligence *(buddhi)*. And the five Pandavas are the five senses brought under its control. And it is indeed desirable that they are so controlled. Since all the five senses were under the control of the mind and had become refined, the mind can be said to have wedded to the five senses.

The strength which Draupadi showed was immeasurable. Even Bhima and a noble king like Yudhishthir were afraid of her.

I read Draupadi's prayer in the Mahabharata when I was in prison and I cried for a long time. To my mind this prayer of Draupadi has extraordinary strength in it. Countless people recite these verses in North India.

The power of words increases or decreases in proportion to the intensity of spiritual effort underlying them. What is there in the word 'ॐ'? It is simply made up of three letters अ, उ a and म्. And yet its value lies in the spiritual force associated with it. When there is greater penance behind the word, its value becomes greater. The same is the case with Draupadi. She may even be regarded as just another imaginary character created by Vyasji. Such a woman may have actually existed or she may not have. But the great strength of Vyasji's own spiritual stature and the recitation by crores of human beings of the prayers composed by him for Draupadi, have raised the value of that prayer.

Govinda means the master of the senses; by *Gopis* are meant the thousands of sense impulses. 'Gopijanapriya' means one who is the beloved of the many or say, of the weak. Draupadi was hemmed in by the Kauravas. The Kauravas are all our base desires. Draupadi cries out 'Keshava, how is it that you do not know me?' It is the cry of all who are distressed. Do we not all have evil desires? When are we completely free from passions? When Draupadi says that she has been surrounded by Kauravas, 'Kauravas' may also mean wicked persons. But we are oppressed even more by our evil desires than by wicked persons. So it is better to interpret 'Kauravas' to mean evil desires.

Draupadi is a true servant of God and as such she has

the right to chide even Him. She cries, 'Oh Master, Oh Lord, Oh Ramanath, i.e. Lakshmipati, i.e. Lord of the World. He who gives salvation, He who brings about self-realisation, I am drowning in a sea of Kauravas, i.e. I am sinking in a multitude of wild desires; I am full of wicked passions. Save me.'

Draupadi calls out 'Krishna, Krishna'. When a person is either in great joy or in great trouble, he or she thus calls out the name twice. She says, 'I come to you for refuge; save me; I am beset with evil passions, and have become helpless. Raise me out of all this.'

* * *

We are helpless like Draupadi, because we are all full of impurities and evil desires of various kinds. Our fear of snakes and such like is a proof of our weakness. I am regarded as the highest in the shram, but I, too, have these fears. It means that I also am more helpless than Draupadi.

Dwarka in the Gita means the whole world, or our own selves, not the dirty little town near Porbandar in Kathiawa.

* * *

You should give up the idea, "I have no one in the world". God is the help of all. It is possible to throw the blame for the present sorry condition of women on their husbands. But women should only think how best they can cast off their own weakness themselves.

* * *

There can be only one prayer for us all. If we offer this prayer daily, understanding it properly, it will for ever be present in our thoughts. Keshava (God) is always with us. He is not in some place called Dwarka. That is only the language of the poet. Draupadi forgot that Keshava was always present everywhere. He clothed her body again and again while Duryodhana was pulling her clothes off. Whenever evil thoughts or evil desires spring in our mind, we should ask ourselves why such thoughts should come to us and think of these verses.

* * *

If a labourer does all his work dedicating it to God, then he can attain self-realisation. Self-realisation means purity of self. Strictly speaking, only those who do bodily labour achieve self-realisation; because 'God is the strength of the weak'. By 'weak' is not meant 'weak in body', though for them too their strength is God-but we should take it to mean weak in means and equipment. The labourer must cultivate humility. An exclusive development of the intellect may lead to the development of a diabolic kind of intelligence. By doing merely intellectual work, we develop satanic tendencies. It is, for this that the Gita says that lie who eats without doing labour eats stolen food. Humility is inherent in each act of labour. And that is why it is *Karmayoga*, or activity that leads to salvation. Doing physical work simply for getting money is no *Karmayoga*, since the idea is simply to earn money. Cleaning of latrines for earning money is no *yajna* (sacrifice). But the same act, if done by way of service, for the sake of sanitation and for the good of others, becomes *yajna*. One who does physical labour out of a spirit of service, in all humility and for self-realisation, gets self-realisation. Such a person would never feel reluctant to work. He should ever be tireless.

* * *

I would certainly worship an idol even made of clay, if thereby my heart feels lighter. If my life seems satisfying and meaningful, fruitful, then the worship of young Krishna's idol has meaning. The stone is no God; but God resides in the stone. If ever I besmear an idol with sandal-wood paste, make an offering of rice, and pray to it for strength to kill others, I hope one of you will have the strength to pick the idol up and throw it into a well or even break it into pieces.

* * *

If we wish to develop in us the capacity to look on all as equals, we should also aim at getting only what the rest of the world gets. Thus, if the whole world gets milk, we may also have it. We may pray to God and say, "O God, if you wish me to have milk, give it first to the rest of the world." But who can pray thus? Only he who has so much sympathy for others and who labours for their good. Even if we cannot practise this principle, we must at least understand and appreciate it. For the present, our only prayer to God should be that since we are fallen so low he should accept whatever liitle we are capable of doing. Even if we do not progress very far in this direction, he should give us strength to lessen our possessions. If we repent of our sins, they will at least not increase, further. We should not keep anything with us thinking it as our own, but should strive to give up as many of our possessions as we can.

* * *

This body is sometimes called a precious gift. If we remain devoted to God, it will really prove to be a precious possession. But to become wholly devoted to God, we have to control the body.

* * *

Passionate desire is common both to man and woman. The mind of such a person always wanders about seeking an object of pleasure. But we must understand that we have obtained this birth not for enjoying or giving such pleasures, but for self-realisation.

* * *

Our temple is in our Ashram; why, it is in our hearts. A temple constructed out of a few stones has no meaning. Only a temple raised in our hearts has any use.

If our Ashram goes on well like this, and does not produce any bad people within it, it would become a place of pilgrimage.

* * *

Every pebble on the bank of the Narmada is said to be Shiva. By the Narmada we do not mean only the river near Broach, but all rivers. If we wash clean a pebble on the bank of a river and offer a *bilvapatra*[1] to it, the pebble becomes Shiva for us. Going a step further, if we take a lump of earth and mould it to the shape of a Shiva-idol, it also becomes Shiva for us. On the same lines, we may have the faith that Shiva resides in the hearts of us all. We are idol-worshippers as well as idol-breakers simultaneously. We are to break what is. mere matter in an idol, but to worship the divine spirit within it.

* * *

Devotees of God carry on activities dictated by their inner voice. But the inner voice also can sometimes. deceive us. So devotees must alway remain vigilant.

* * *

There is no meaning in our observing sacred days and vows without understanding their significance. Such observance becomes useful both to us and to society if we understand its meaning and can explain it to others. Our women observe Nagapanchami, Janmashtami, and other holy days. But they should understand why they are observing them. It is possible that the meaning of Nagapanchami is to regard the serpent as the symbol of one's enemy and it was sought through this means to inculcate the principle that one should not kill even one's enemy. In this world, there is no other creature so poisonous to man as a serpent except another man. If we find anyone as full of venom as a serpent, we should learn to love him, as though he were full of nectar. From doing this, we shall learn that every human being is worthy of war hip, i.e. of service.

* * *

Instead of training women to use a dagger, it is better to teach them to be fearless. God's protecting hands are always over us. If we really believe in the existence of God, whom shall we fear? Even if the most wicked of persons assaults you, take Ramanama (the name of God). Most wicked persons would run away at this earnest cry to God. But if that does not happen, what does it matter? We should learn to die on such an occasion.[99]

SECTION III

Ramanama

Even if you do nothing else, keep repeating Ramanama. Some day you will suddenly see light in the midst of darkness.

*

Even if I am killed, I will not give up repeating the names of Rama and Rahim which mean to' me the Same God. With these names on my lips I would die cheerfully.

*

I am longing to disappear from the world quietly with Ramanama on my lips.

A Good Seed Sown

From my sixth or seventh year up to my sixteenth I was at school, being taught all sorts of things except religion. I may say that I failed to get from the teachers what they could have given me without any effort on their part. And yet I kept on picking up things here and there from my surroundings. The term *religion* I am using in its broadest sense, meaning thereby self-realization or knowledge of self.

Being born in the Vaishnava faith, I had often to go to the *haveli*. But it never appealed to me. I did not like its glitter and pomp. Also I heard rumours of immorality being practised there, and lost all interest in it. Hence, I could gain nothing from the *haveli*.

But what I failed to get there I obtained from my nurse, an old servant of the family, whose affection for me I still recall. There was in me a fear of ghosts and spirits. Rambha, for that was her name, suggested, as a remedy for this fear, the repetition of Ramanama. I had more faith in her than in her remedy, and so at a tender age I began repeating Ramanama to cure my fear of ghosts and spirits. This was, of course, short-lived; but the good seed sown in childhood was not sown in vain. I think it is due to the seed sown by that good woman Rambha that today Ramanama is an infallible remedy for me.[1]

Who is Rama?

You ask what is Rama. I may explain to you the meaning of that word, but then your repetition of that name would be nearly fruitless. But if you understand that Rama is He whom you intend to worship and then repeat His name, it will serve the purpose of the horn of plenty for you. You may repeat it like a parrot, but still it will be helpful because your repetition unlike the parrot's is backed by a purpose. Thus you do not need any symbol, and Tulsidas holds that the name

Ramanama **121**

of Rama is more powerful than Rama himself and suggests that there is no relation between the word Rama and its meaning. The meaning will be filled in later by the devotee in accordance with the nature of his devotion. That is the beauty .of this repetition *(japa)*. Otherwise it would be impossible to prove that it will make a new man even of a simpleton. The devotee must fulfil only a single condition. The name should not be repeated for show or with a view to deceiving others, but with determination and faith. If a man perseveres with such. repetition, I have not the shadow of a doubt that it will be for him a universal provider. Every one who has the requisite patience can realize this in his own case. For days and sometimes for years, the mind wanders and becomes restless, the body craves for sleep when one is engaged in repeating the name. Indeed even still more painful symptoms intervene. Still if the seeker perseveres with the repetition, it is bound to bear fruit. Spinning is a gross material accomplishment and yet it can be acquired only after our patience is sorely tried. Things more difficult than spinning demand a greater effort on our part. Therefore he who is out to attain the Supreme must undergo the necessary discipline for a long, long time and never be downhearted. I think I have now answered all your questions. If you have faith, repeat the name at all times, when you sit or stand or lie down, eat or drink. There is no reason to despair if the whole of your life-time is spent while you are at it. If you try it, you will have peace of mind in an increasing measure from day to day.[2]

Q.: You have often said that when you talk of Rama you refer to the ruler of the universe and not to Rama, the son of Dasharatha. But we find that your Ramadhun calls on 'Sita-Rama', 'Raja Rama' and it ends with 'Victory to Rama, the Lord of Sita'. Who is this Rama if not the son of the King Dasharatha?

A.: I have answered such questions before. But there is something new in this one. It demands a reply. In Ramadhun 'Raja Rama', 'Sita-Rama' are undoubtedly repeated. Is not this Rama the same as the son of Dasharatha? Tulsidas has answered this question. But let me put down my own view. More potent than Rama is the Name. Hindu Dharma is like a boundless ocean teeming with priceless gems. The deeper you dive the more treasures you find. In Hindu religion God is known by various names. Thousands of people look doubtless upon Rama and Krishna as historical figures and literally believe that God came down in person on earth in the form of Rama, the son of Dasharatha, and by worshipping him one can attain salvation. The same thing holds good about Krishna. History, imagination and truth have got so inextricably mixed up. It is next to impossible to disentangle them. I have accepted all the names and forms attributed to God, as symbols connoting one formless omnipresent Rama. To me, therefore, Rama, described as the Lord of Sita, son of Dasharatha, is the all powerful essence whose name, inscribed in the heart, removes all suffering, mental, moral and physical.[3]

Power of Ramanama

What, then, does this Ramanama mean? Is it something to be repeated parrot-like? Certainly not. If that were so, all of us would win deliverance by repeating it mechanically. Ramanama ought to be repeated from the depth of one's heart; it would not then matter if the words are not pronounced correctly. The broken words which proceed from the heart are acceptable in God's court. Even though the heart cries out "*Mara, mara*" (Rama pronounced wrongly, i.e. in the reverse and then meaning "dying, dying"), this appeal of the heart will be recorded in one's credit column. On the contrary, though the tongue may pronounce the name of Rama correctly, if the lord of that heart is Ravana, the correct repetition of Rama's name will be recorded in one's debit column.

Tulsidas did not sing the glory of Ramanama for the benefit of the hypocrite who "has Rama's name on his lips and a knife under his arm". His wise calculations will go wrong, while the seeming errors of the man who has installed Rama in his heart will succeed. Rama alone can repair one's fortunes and so the poet Surdas, lover of God, sings :

Who will repair my fortunes?

O who else but Rama?
Everyone is a friend of his on whom good fortune smiles,
None of his whom fortune has forsaken.

The reader, therefore, should understand clearly that Ramanama is a matter of the heart. Where speech and the mind are not in harmony with each other, mere speech is falsehood, no more than pretence or play of words. Such chanting may well deceive the world, but can Rama who dwells in man's heart be deceived? Hanuman broke open the beads in the necklace which Sita gave him as a gift, wanting to see whether they were inscribed with Rama's name. Some courtiers who thought themselves wise asked him why he showed disrespect to Sita's necklace. Hanuman's reply was that—if the beads were not inscribed with Rama's name inside, then every necklace given to him by Sita was a burden to him. The wise courtiers thereupon smilingly asked him if Rama's name was inscribed in his heart. Hanuman drew out his knife and, cutting open his chest, said : "Now look inside. Tell me if you see anything else there except Rama's name". The courtiers felt ashamed. Flowers rained on Hanuman from the sky, and from that day Hanuman's name is always invoked when Rama's story is recited.

This may be only a legend or a dramatist's invention. Its moral is valid for all time : only that which is in one's heart is true.[4]

But for one who has never experienced peace and is in quest of it, Ramanama will certainly prove a *parasmani* (philosopher's stone). God has been given a thousand names which only means that He can be called by any name and that His qualities are infinite. That is why God is also beyond nomenclature and free from attributes, But for us mortals the support of His name is absolutely essential to fall back upon and in this age even the ignorant and the illiterate can have recourse to an *Ekakshara mantra* (Om) in the form of Ramanama. In fact, uttering Ramanama covers the *Ekakshara* and there is no difference between 'Om' and 'Rama'. But the value of reciting His name cannot be established by reasoning, it can only be experienced if one does it with faith.[5]

If you repeat the name of Rama on getting up in the

morning and before going to bed in the evening the day will go well for you and the night pass without bad dreams.⁶

A Well-tried Formula

It is easy enough to take a vow under a stimulating influence. But it is difficult to keep to it especially in the midst of temptation. God is our only help in such circumstances. I therefore suggested to the meeting (of elders at Vedchhi in Surat district) Ramanama. Rama, Allah and God are to me convertible terms. I had discovered that simple people deluded themselves in the belief that I appeared to them in their distress. I wanted to remove the superstition. I knew that I appeared to nobody. It was pure hallucination for them to rely on a frail mortal. I therefore presented them with a simple and well-tried formula that has never failed, namely to invoke the assistance of God every morning before sunrise, and every evening before bed time, for the fulfilment of the vows. Millions of Hindus know him under the name of Rama. As a child I was taught to call upon Rama when I was seized with fear. I know many of my companions to whom Ramanama has been of the greatest solace in the hour of their need. I presented it to the Dharalas (A fierce, military tribe in Gujarat whose occupation is chiefly farming) and to the untouchables. I present it a whose vision is not blurred and whose faced by overmuch learning. Learning takes stages in life but it fails us utterly in the and temptation. Then faith alone save not for those who tempt God in every v ever expect it to save. It is for those 'fear of God, who want to restrain themselves and cannot in spite of themselves.⁷

Ridiculing Ramanama

Q.: You know, we are so ignorant and dull that we actually begin to worship the images of our great men instead of living up to their teachings. *Ramalila, Krishnalila* and the recently opened Gandhi temple are a living testimony of that. The Ramanama bank in Banaras and wearing clothes printed with Ramanama is, in my opinion, a caricature and even insult of Ramanama. Don't you think that under these circumstances your telling the people to take to Ramanama as a sovereign remedy for all ailments is likely to encourage ignorance and hypocrisy? Ramanama repeated from the heart can be a sovereign remedy, but in my opinion religious education of the right type alone can lead to that state.

A.: You are right. There is so much superstition and hypocrisy around that one is afraid even to do the right thing. But if one gives way to fear, even truth will have to be suppressed. The golden rule is to act fearlessly upon what one believes to be right. Hypocrisy and untruth will go on in the world. Our doing the right thing will result in their decrease if any, never in their increase. The danger is that when we are surrounded by falsehood on all sides we might be caught in it and begin to deceive ourselves. We should be careful not to make a mistake out of our laziness and ignorance. Constant vigilance under all circumstances is essential. A votary of truth cannot act otherwise. Even an all-power remedy like Ramanama can become useless for lack of wakefulness and care, and become one more addition to the numerous current superstitions.[8]

Ramanama Must Not Cease

Q.: While in conversation or doing brain work or when one is suddenly worried, can one recite Ramanama in one's heart? Do people do so at such times, and if so, how?

A.: Experience shows that man can do so at any time, even in sleep provided Ramanama is enshrined in his heart. If the taking of the name has become a habit, its recitation through the heart becomes as natural as the heart beat. Otherwise, Ramanama is a mere mechanical performance or at best has touched the heart only on the surface. When

Ramanama has established its dominion over the heart, the question of vocal recitation does not arise. Because then it transcends speech. But it may well be held that persons who have attained this state are few and far between.

There is no doubt whatsoever that Ramanama contains all the power that is attributed to it. No one can, by mere wishing, enshrine Ramanama in his heart. Untiring effort is required as also patience. What an amount of labour and patience have been lavished by men to acquire the non-existence philosopher's stone? Surely, God's name is of infinitely richer value and always existent.

Q.: Is it harmful if, owing to stress or exigencies of work, one is unable to carry out daily devotions in the prescribed manner? Which of the two should be given preference? Service or the rosary?

A.: Whatever the exigencies of service or adverse circumstances may be, Ramanama must not cease. The outward form will vary according to the occasion. The absence of the rosary does not interrupt Ramanama which has found an abiding place in the heart.[9]

Ramanama and National Service

Q.: Can a man or woman attain self-realization by mere recitation of Ramanama and without taking part in national service? I ask this question because some of my sisters say that they do not need to do anything beyond attending to family requirements, and occasionally showing kindness to the poor.

A.: This question has puzzled not only women, but many men, and has taxed me to the utmost. I know that there is a school of philosophy which teaches complete inaction and futility of all effort. I have not been able to appreciate that teaching, unless in order to secure verbal agreement I were to put my own interpretation on it. In my humble opinion, effort *is* necessary for one's own growth. It has to be irrespective of results. Ramanama or some equivalent is necessary, not for the sake of repetition, but for the sake of purification, as an aid to effort, for direct guidance from above. It is, therefore, never a substitute for effort. It is meant for intensifying and guiding it in proper channel. If all effort is vain, why family cares or an occasional help to the poor? In this very effort is contained the germ of national service. And national service, to me, means service of humanity, even as disinterested service of the family means the same thing. Disinterested service of the family, necessarily, leads one to national service. Ramanama gives one detachment and ballast, and never throws one off one's balance at critical moments. Self-realization I hold to be impossible without service of, and identification with, the poorest.[10]

Ramanama

To think of God as 'God' does not fire me as the name Rama does. There is all the poetry in it. I know that my forefathers have known him as Rama. They have been uplifted for Rama, and when I take the name of Rama, I arise with the same energy. It would not be possible for me to use the name 'God' as it is written in the Bible. It is so contrary to experience. I should not be lifted to the truth. Therefore my whole soul rejects the teaching that Rama is not my God.'[11]

Hanuman tore open his heart and showed that there was nothing there but Ramanama. I have none of the power of Hanuman to tear open my heart, but if any one of you feel inclined to do it, I assure you will find nothing here but love for Rama whom I see face to face in the starving millions of India.[12]

REFERENCES

Section I
1. *Young India*, 10-6-'26, p. 211
2. *Young India*, 16-12-'26, p. 440
3. *The Collected Works of Mahatma Gandhi*-XLIX (1972), p.222
4. *Harijan*, 5-1-'47, p. 479
5. *The Collected Works of Mahatma Gandhi*-XI, (1964), p. 126
6. *Hind Swaraj*, (1962), p. 71
7. *Harijan*, 18-4-'36, p. 77
8. *Harijan*, 3-3-'46, p. 29
9. *Bapu's Letters to Mira* [1924-1948], (1959), p. 286
10. *Harijan*, 28-4-'46, p. III
11. *Young India*, 23-1-'30, p. 25
12. *The Collected Works of Mahatma Gandhi.-XXV*, (1967), p. 321
13. *Mahadevbhaini Diary*, Vol. 2 (Gujarati Edn., 1949), p. 114
14. *The Collected Works of Mahatma Gandhi-XXXII, (1969)*, p. 219-20
15. *The Diary of Mahadev Desai*, Vol. I, (1953), p. 222
16. *The Collected Works of Mahatma Gandhi-XLIV, (1971)*, p.85
17. *Young India*, 15-12-'27, p. 424
18. *Food for the Soul*, (1957), pp. 59-60
19. *The Collected Works of Mahatma Gandhi-XLVIII (1972)*, p.11
20. *Harijan*, 18-8-'46 p. 267
21. *Harijan*, 26-5-'46, p. 156
22. *Food for the Soul*, (1957), p. 80 fn.
23. *Food for the Soul*, (1957), p. 80
24. *Food for the Soul*, (1957), p. 62
25. *Young India*, 7-1-'32, p. 8
26. *Bapu's Letters to Ashram Sisters*, (1960), p. 28
27. *Harijan*, 5-5-'46, p. 113
28. *Harijan*, 25-5-'35, p. 115
29. *The Collected Works of Mahatma Gandhi*-L, (1972), p. 326
30. *Young India*, 23-9-'26, p. 333
31. *Young India*, 14-10-'26, p. 358
32. *Mahadevbhaini Diary*, Vol. 2, (Gujarati Edn. 1949), p. 24
33. *Mahatma Gandhi—The Last Phase* Vol. I, Book One (1965), p. 59

34. *The Collected Works of Mahatma Gandhi*—XXXII, (1969), p. 35
35. *The Collected Works of Mahatma Gandhi*—XL VII, (1971), p. 326
36. *The Collected Works of Mahatma Gandhi*—XLIV, (1971), p. 333
37. *Young India*, 17-6-'26, p. 215
38. *An Autobiography*, (1969), pp. 52-54
39. *Young India*, 4-4-'29, p. 110
40. *Harijan*, 1-6-'35, p. 123.
41. *Young India*, 30-8-'28, p. 291
42. *Harijan*, 22-2-'42, p. 47
43. *An Autobiaoraplry*, (1969), p. 238
44. *The Collected Works of Mahatma Gandhi*—L, (1972), pp. 377-78
45. *Young India*, 5-6-'24, p. 187
46. *Bapu's Letters to Mira* [1924-1948], (1959), p. 255
47. *Harijan*, 23-7 '38, p. 192
48. *Harijan*, 21-4-'46, p. 94
49. *My Memorable Moments with Bapu*, (1960), Ch. 25, p. 46
50. *Harijan*, 8-6-'35, p. 132
51. *Harijan*, 15-6-'35, p. 140
52. *Harijan;* 2-2-'34, p. 5
53. *The Collected Works of Mahatma Gandhi*—L, (1972), p. 326
54. *Homage to the Departed* (1958), p. 202

Section II
1. *Harijan*, 3-5-' 42, p. 139
2. *Harijan*, 8-5-'37, p. 99
3. *Harijan*, 24-12-'38, p. 395
4. *The Collected Works of Mahatma Gandhi*—XXXI, (1969,) p. 542
5. *An Autobiography*, (1969), p. 118
6. *Ibid.*, Introduction, p. x
7. *Young India*, 14-8-'24, p. 267.
8. *The Collected Works of Mahatma Gandhi*—XXIII, (1967), p. 289
9. *Bapu's Letters to the Ashram Sisters*, (1960), p. 79

10. *Mahadevbhaini Diary*, Vol. 2, (Gujarati Edn.1949), p.161
11. *Ibid.*, p. 243
12. *The Collected Works of Mahatma Gandhi*-XLIV, (1971), p. 367
13. *Young India*, 14-2-'29, p. 51
14. *Harijan*, 13-10-'46; p. 357
15. *Harijan*, 20-4-'35, p. 74
16. *The Diary of Mahadev Desai*, Vol. I, (1953), p. 233
17. *Harijan*, 7-7-'46, p. 216
18. *Speeches and Writings of Mahatma Gandhi*, (G. A. Natesan & Co., 4th Edn.), p. 1066
19. *Young India*, 24-9-'25, p. 331
20. *Harijan*, 18-8-'46, p. 265
21. *Young India*, 29-12–'27, p. 444
22. *The Diary of Mahadev Desai*, Vol. I, (1953), pp. 232-33)
23. *Stray Glimpses of Bapu*, (1960), pp. 112-14
24. *Harijan*, 16-6-'46, p. 183
25. *The End of An Epoch*, (1962), p. 41
26. *Bapu's Letters to Ashram Sisters*, (1960), p. 3
27. *Ibid*, p. 48
28. *The Collected Works of Mahatma Gandhi*—L, (1972), pp. 133-34
29. *The Collected Works of Mahatma Gandhi*-XXXII, (1969), p. 201
30. *The Collected Works of Mahatma Gandhi*—XLIX, (1972), p. 71
31. *The Collected Works of Mahatma Gandhi* XXXVIII, (1970), p. 197
32. *The Collected Works of Mahatma Gandhi*—XLV, (1971), pp. 21-22
33. *The Collected Works of Mahatma Gandhi*—XXXII, (1969), p. 220
34. *"My Dear Child"*, (1959), pp. 45-46
35. *Young India*, 6-8-'25, pp. 274-75
36. *An Autobiography*, (1969), p. 46
37. *Harijan*, 24-9-'38, p. 267
38. *Truth is God*, (1959), p. 53

39. *Bapu—My Mother* (1955), p. 46
40. *Harijan*, 10-12-'38, p. 373
41. *Young India*, 22-9-'27, p. 321.
42. *The Collected Works of Mahatma Gandhi*—XLIX, (1972), p. 455
43. *Harijan*, 5-11-'38, p. 317
44. *Food for the Soul*, (1957), p. 55
45. *The Collected Works of Mahatma Gandhi,*—XXXVIII, (1970), p.281
46. *Harijan*, 19-5-'46, p. 135
47. *The Diary of Mahadev Desai*, Vol. I, (1953), pp. 312-13.
48. *Harijan*, 28-4-'46, p. 112
49. *Harijan*, 7-4-'46, p. 73
50. *Harijan*, 3-3-'46, pp. 25-26
51. *Young India*, 8-9-'27, p. 295
52. *Harijan*, 22-9-'46, p. 319
53. *Food for the Soul*, (1957), pp. 63-64
54. *Food for the Soul*, (1957), pp. 61-62
55. *The Collected Works of Mahatma Gandhi-L*, (1972), pp. 245-46
56. *Ibid.*, p. 136
57. *The Collected Works of Mahatma Gandhi*—LI, (1972), p. 304
58. *The Collected Works of Mahatma Gandhi*—XLIX, (1972), p. 455
59. *The Collected Works of Mahatma Gandhi*—XLIX (1972), p. 446
60. *Harijan*, 13-7-'40, p. 194
61. *Harijan*, 11-5-'47, p. 147
62. *Harijan*, 18-3-'39, p. 56
63. *Young India*, 18-4-1929, p. 126
64. *Young India*, 25-9-1924, p. 319J
65. *Harijan*, 8-7-'33, p. 4
66. *Harijan*, 10-4-1937, p. 68
67. *Young India*, 24-3-1920, p. 1
68. *The Collected Works of Mahatma Gandhi*—XVI, (1965), p. 207

69. From Gujarati: *Navajivan*, 12-10-'19] Ibid., pp. 230, 231
70. *Harijan*, 15-4-'33, p. 4
71. *Harijan*, 4-3-'33, p. 8
72. *Harijan*, 11-2-'33, p. 2
73. *Young India*, 23-10-'24, p. 354
74. *Bapu's Letters to Mira* [1924-1948], (1959), p. 251
75. *The End of an Epoch*, (1962), p. 25
76. *The Diary of Mahadev Desai*, Vol. 1, (1953), pp. 168-69
77. *The Gita According to Gandhi*, (1956), pp. 308-09
78. *Young India*, 6-10-'21, p. 318
79. *Young India*, 8-7-'26, p. 24
80. *Harijan*, 9-3-'40, p. 30
81. *Young India*, 5-11-'25, p. 378
82. *Harijan*, 11-3-'33, p.4
83. *Young India*, 4-11-'26, p. 386
84. *The Collected Works of Mahatma Gandhi-LI*, (1972), p. 10
85. Ibid., p. 89
86. *Harijan*, 29-4-33, p. 6
87. *Young India*, 8-12-'27, p. 414
88. *Young India*, 26-9-'29, p. 320
89. *The Collected Works of Mahatma Gandhi—IX*, (1963), pp. 276-77
90. *Ashram Observances in Action*, (1959), Chap. II
91. *Harijan*, 15-2-'42, p. 44
92. *Harijan*, 17-8-'47, p. 281
93. *The Collected Works of Mahatma Gandhi—XXXVI*, (1970), pp. 304-05
94. *The Collected Works of Mahatma Gandhi—XLIX*, (1972), pp. 455-56
95. Ibid, p. 215
96. *The Collected Works of Mahatma Gandhi—L*, (1972). pp. 68-69
97. *The Diary of Mahadev Desai*, Vol. I (1953), p. 219
98. *The Collected Works of Mahatma Gandhi—XLIX*, (1972), p. 406
99. *Bapu's Letters to Ashram Sisters*, (1960), pp. 94-114

Section III
1. *An Autobiography,* (1969), pp. 22-23
2. *The Diary of Mahadev Desai,* Vol. I, (1953), pp. 120-21
3. *Harijan,* 2-6-'46, p. 158
4. *The Collected Works of Mahatma Gandhi—XXVII,* (1968), pp. 111-12
5. *The Collected Works of Mahatma Gandhi—XXXIV,* (1969), pp. 162-63
6. *The Collected Works of Mahatma Gandhi—XXVI,* (1967), p. 7
7. *Young India,* 22-1-'25, p. 26
8. *Harijan,* 2-6-'46, p. 160
9. *Harijan,* 17-2-'46, p. 12
10. *Young India,* 21-10-'26, p. 364
11. *The Collected Works of Mahatma Gandhi-XLVIII,* (1971), p. 127
12. *Young India,* 24-3-'27, p. 23

❏❏❏